These comics and sketches were created in the Spring 2015 Advanced Making Comics Workshop as taught by Professor Lynda Barry, AKA Professor Hebdo.

Featured cartoonists in alphabetical order:

Altaïr
Bulma
Captain Haddock
Companion Cube
Dangermouse
Felicity Merriman
Huck Finn
Hypatia
Knuckles Hemingway
Mafalda
Optimus Prime
Percy
Santa
Sharkbait
Smaug
Scott Pilgrim
Spot
Squilliam Fancyson
Starfire
Superone

Some sketches may belong to unidentified cartoonists.

NULLA DIES SINE LINEA

Published independently by the UW Comics Club.
January 2016. The University of Wisconsin, Madison.
Arranged for publication by Joshua Duncan.

Contact the UW Comics Club Captains via email: comicsclubuw@gmail.com.
See more work at comicsclubuwmadison.tumblr.com.

YOUR ASSIGNMENT:

3 minutes

TO DRAW
OLD MUTHA
HUBBARD
and her
NAUGHTY LITTLE
DOG. MAKING COMICS 2

SHE WENT TO A FRAT PARTY

WEARING A TOGA

WHEN SHE CAME BACK

HE WAS PRACTICING YOGA.

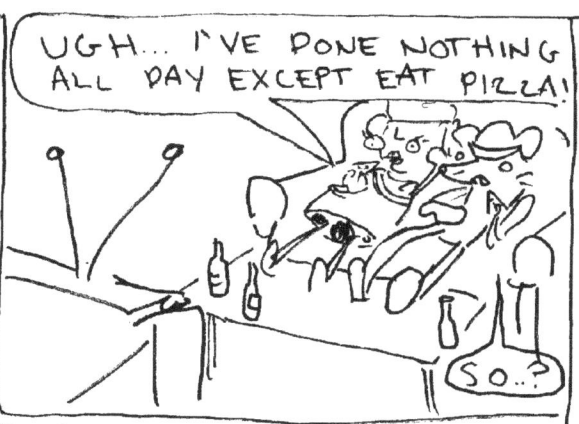

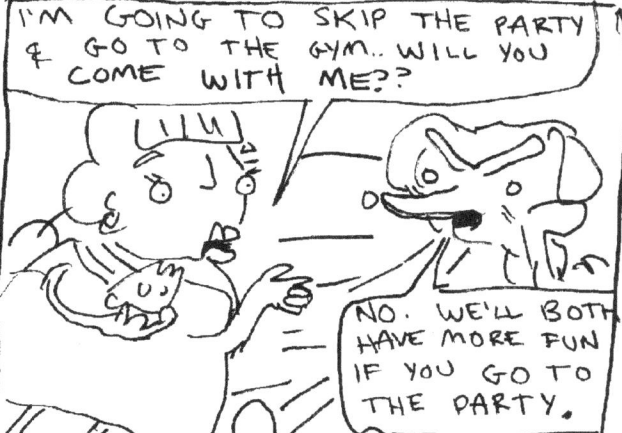

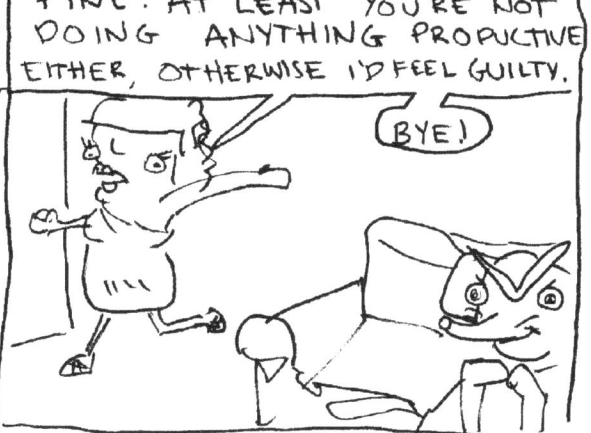

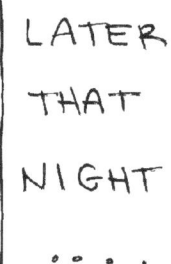

LATER

THAT

NIGHT

. . . .

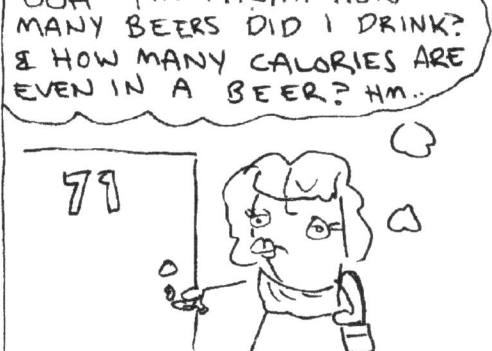

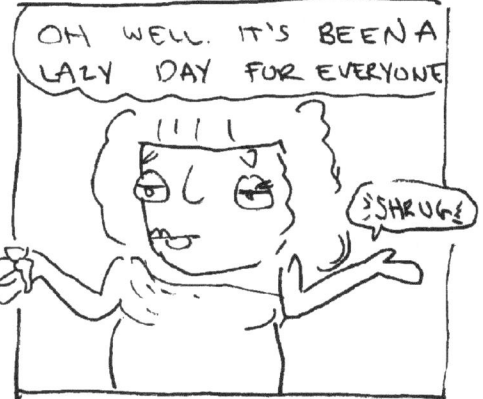

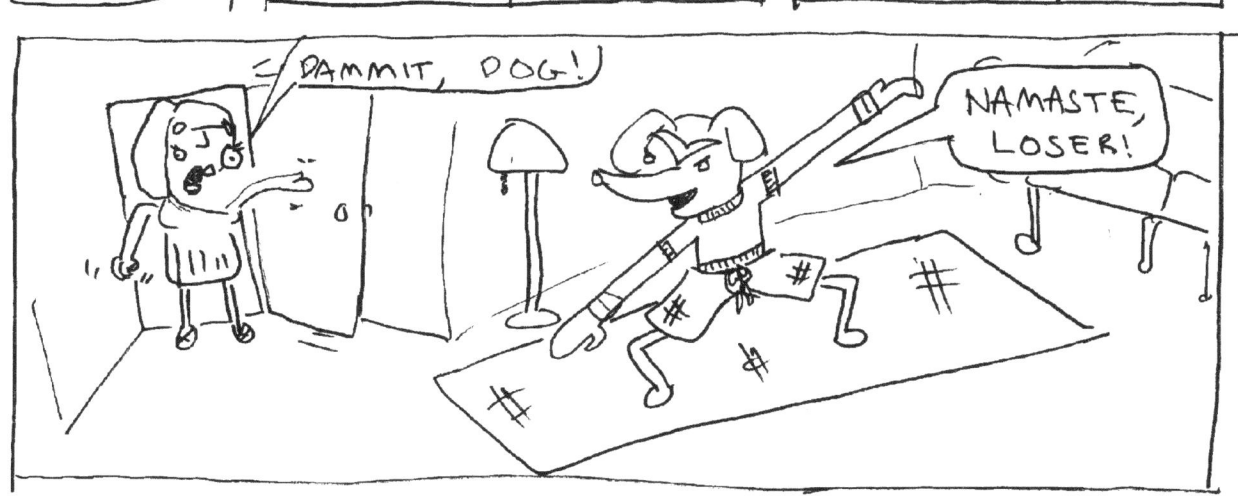

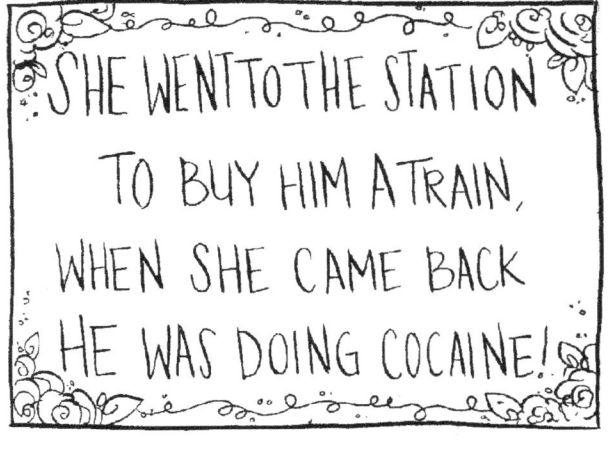

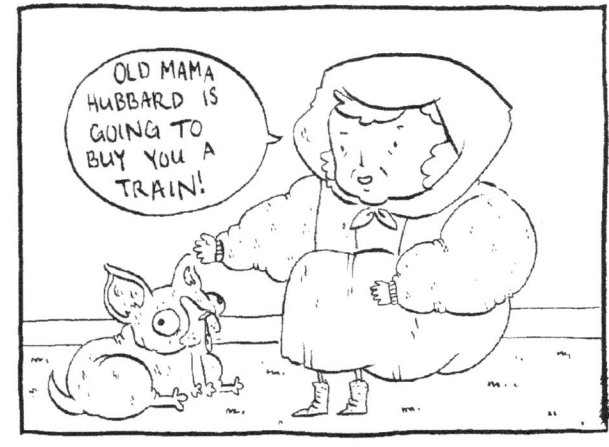

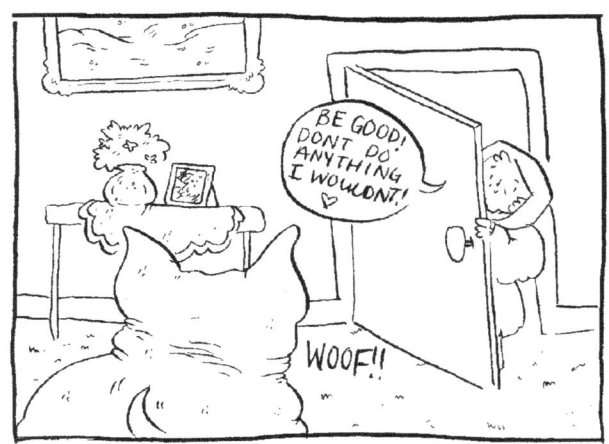

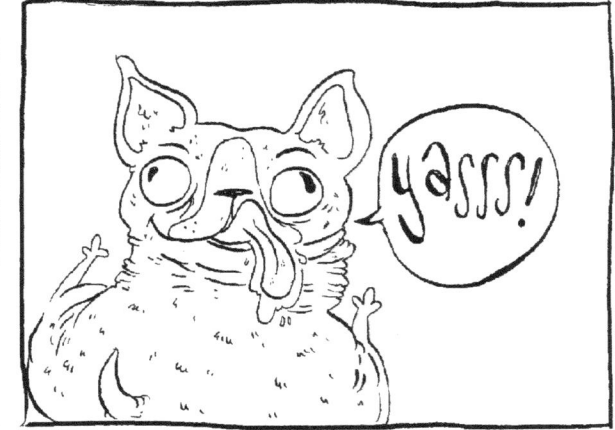

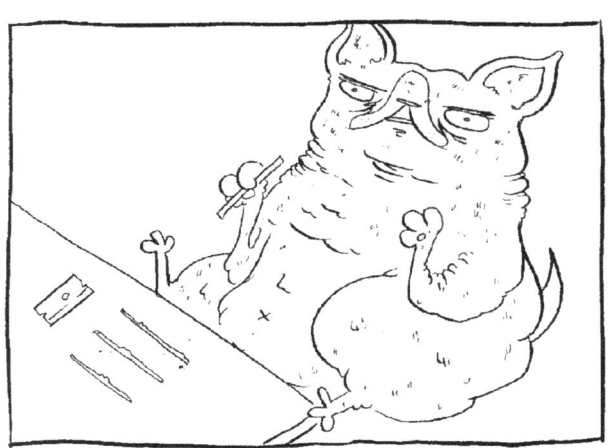

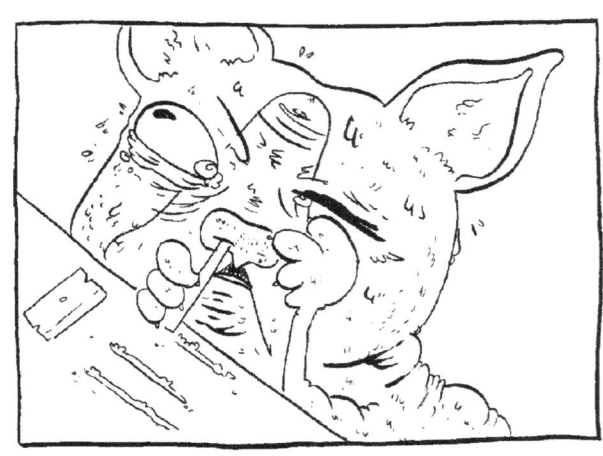

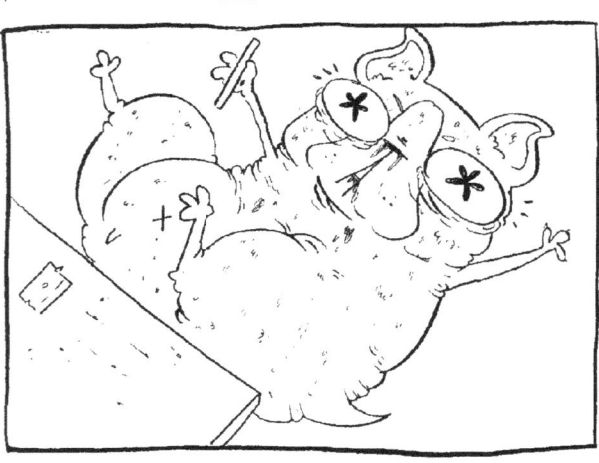

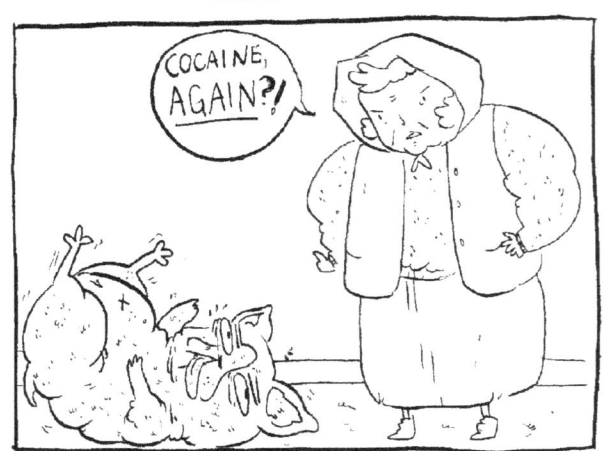

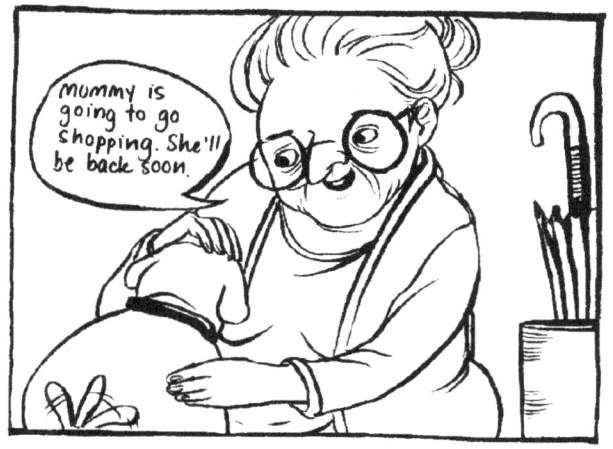

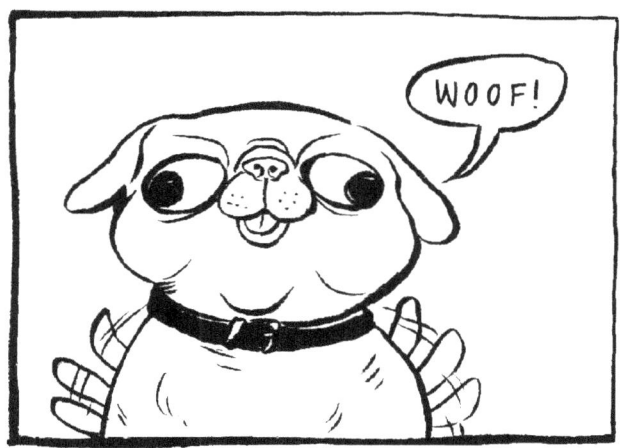

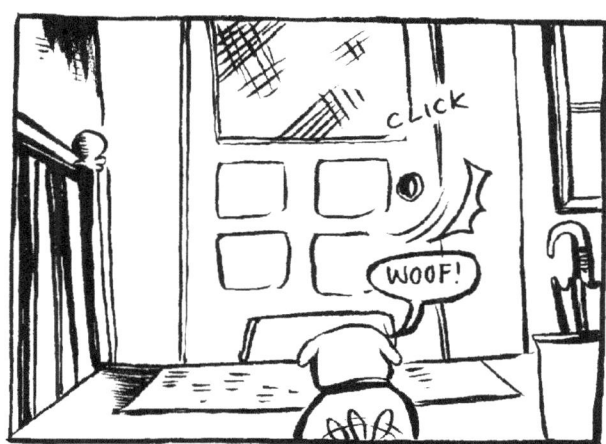

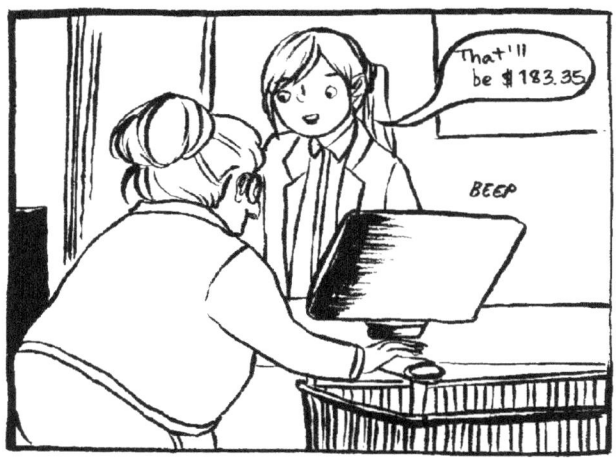

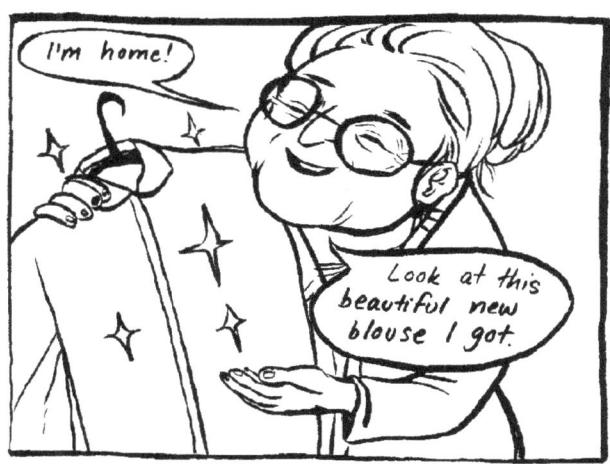

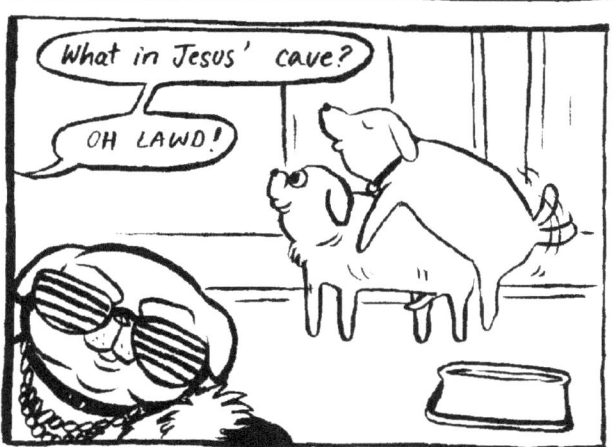

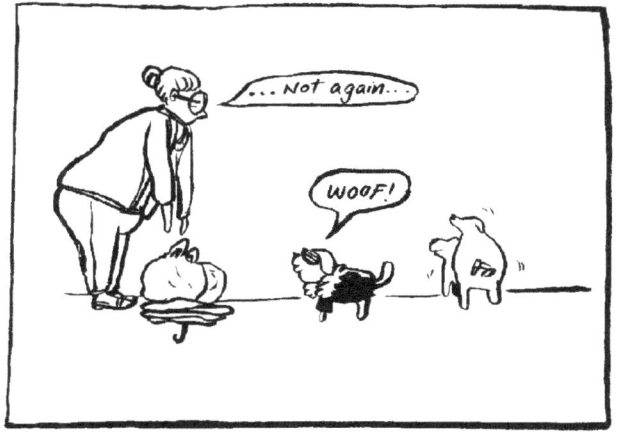

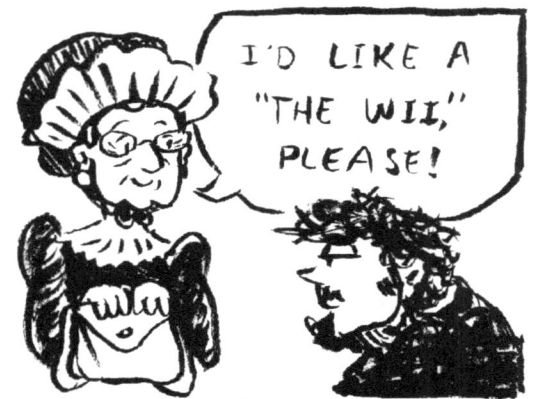
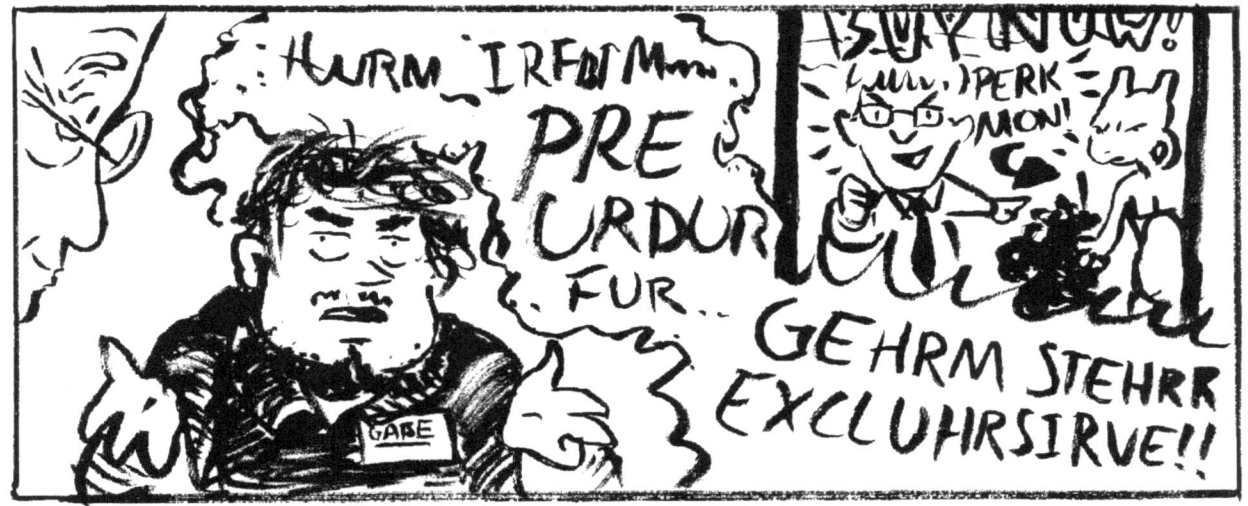
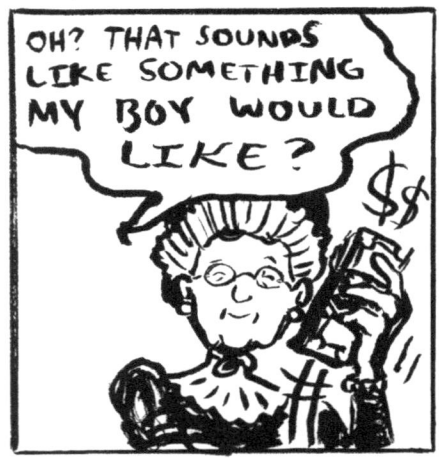
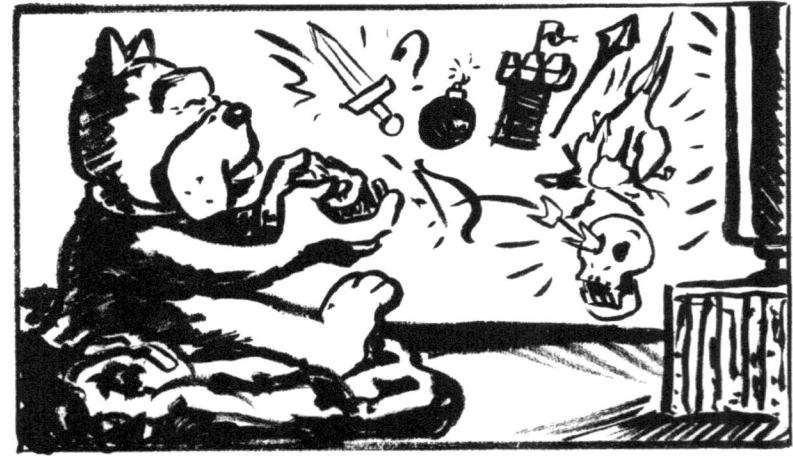
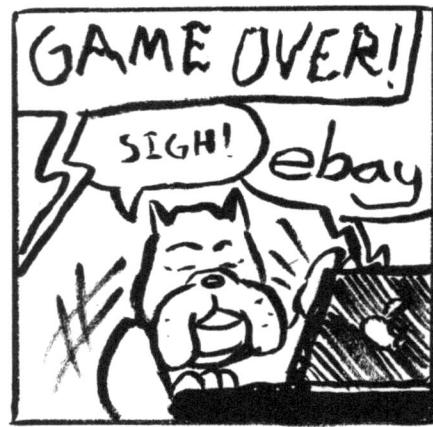
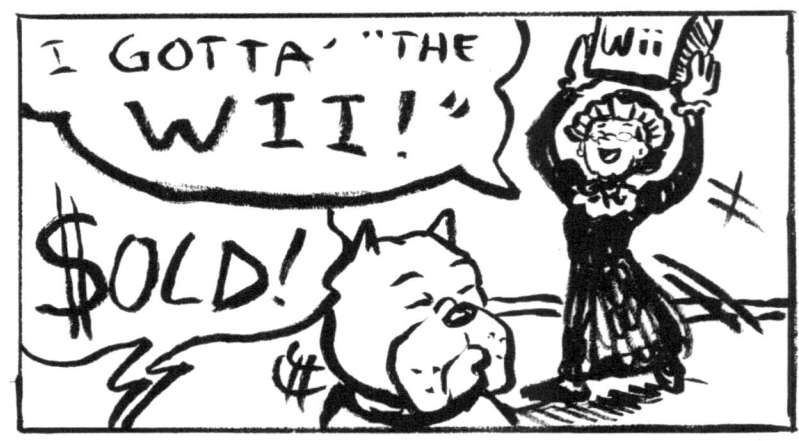

SHE WENT FOR HER AX
WHICH WAS OUT IN THE SHED,
BUT WHEN SHE CAME BACK
HE HAD CRUSHED THE
BEASTS HEAD.

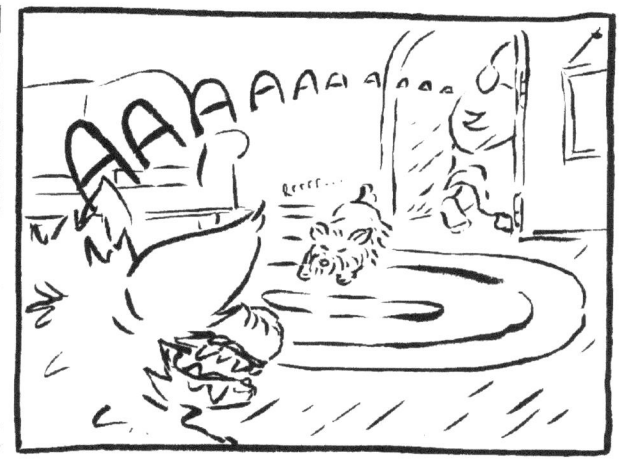

I told the ALPHA's LAST MESSENGER. I WON'T GO BACK TO THE PACK. — LEAVE HERE NOW AND NEVER RETURN TO THIS PLACE AGAIN. YOU HAVE THIS CHANCE.

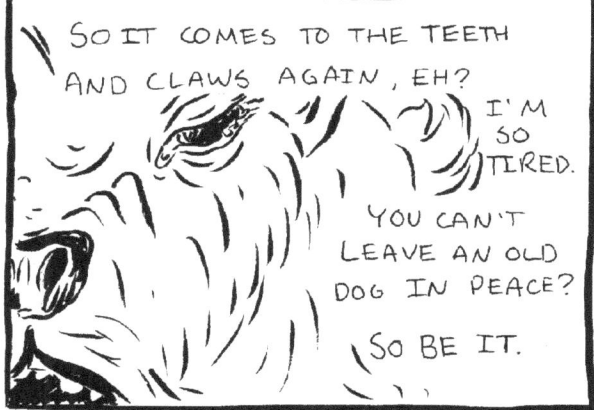

SO IT COMES TO THE TEETH AND CLAWS AGAIN, EH?

I'M SO TIRED.

YOU CAN'T LEAVE AN OLD DOG IN PEACE?

SO BE IT.

YOU SHOULD KNOW BEST OLD FRIEND! I AM NO MESSENGER. — NO ONE LEAVES THE PACK THAT EASILY. NOT EVEN YOU. HAHA!!

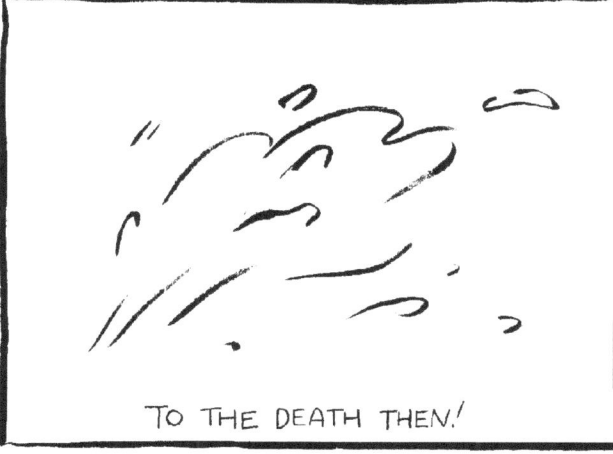

TO THE DEATH THEN!

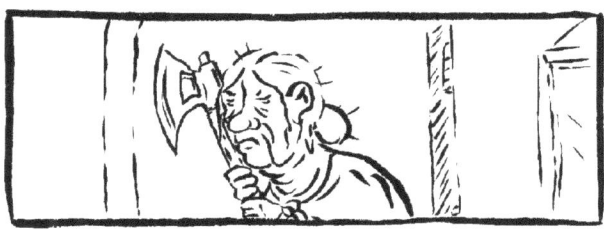

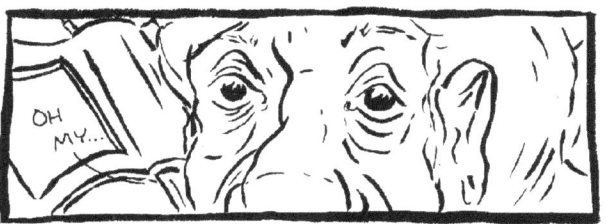

OH MY...

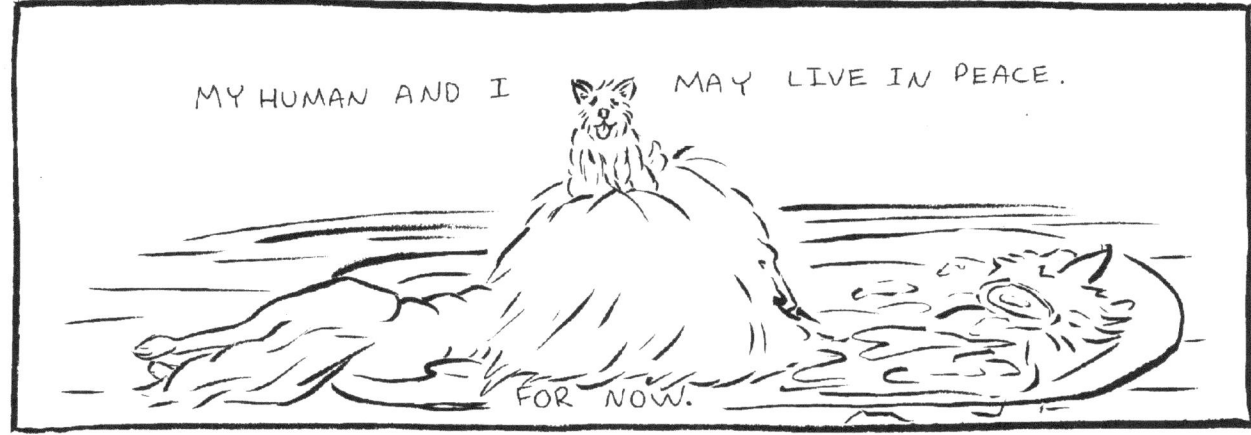

MY HUMAN AND I   MAY LIVE IN PEACE.

FOR NOW.

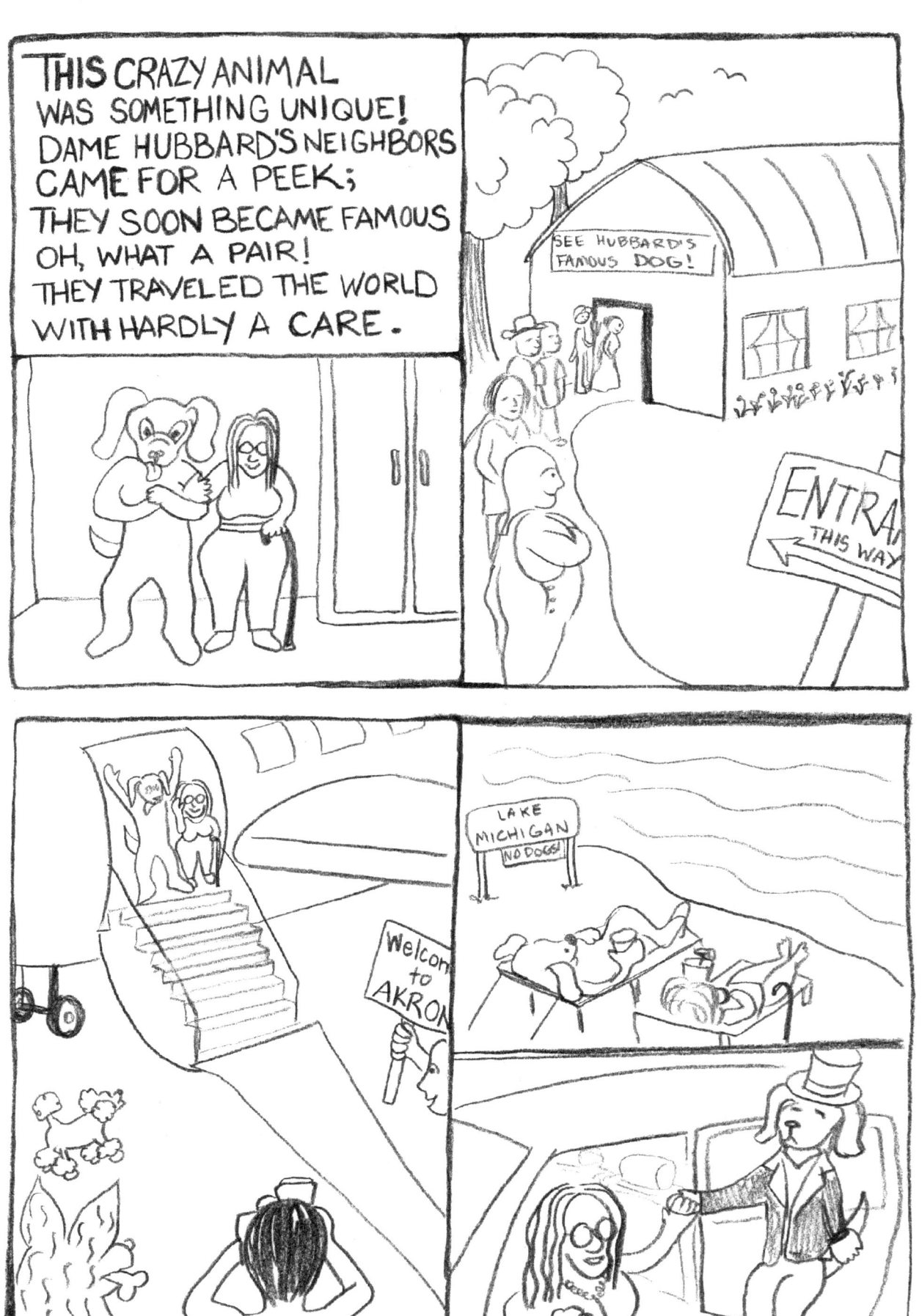

THIS CRAZY ANIMAL
WAS SOMETHING UNIQUE!
DAME HUBBARD'S NEIGHBORS
CAME FOR A PEEK;
THEY SOON BECAME FAMOUS
OH, WHAT A PAIR!
THEY TRAVELED THE WORLD
WITH HARDLY A CARE.

SEE HUBBARD'S FAMOUS DOG!

ENTRA
THIS WAY

LAKE MICHIGAN NO DOGS!

Welcome to AKRON

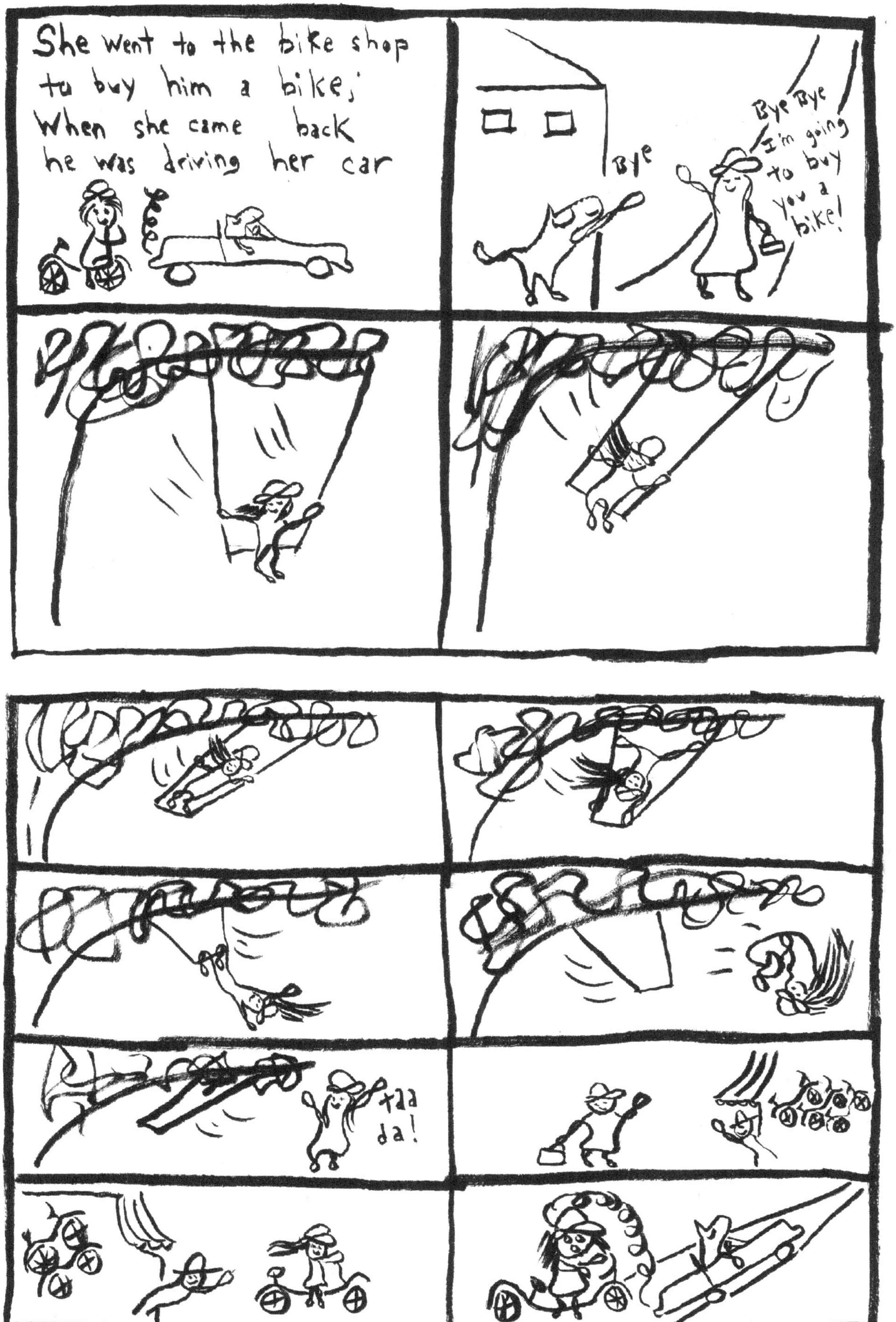

She went to the bike shop to buy him a bike; When she came back he was driving her car

Bye

Bye Bye I'm going to buy you a bike!

taa da!

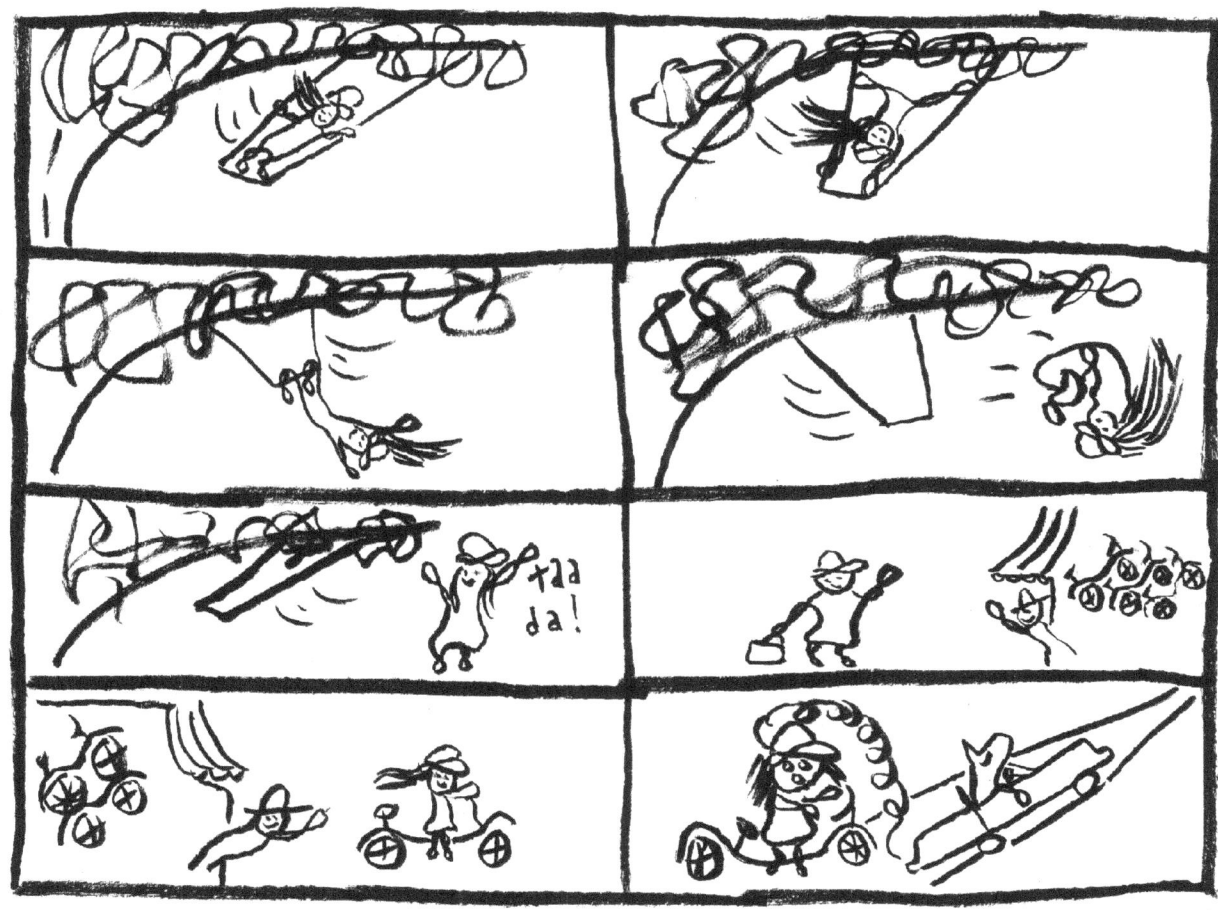

SHE WENT TO THE D.M.V.
BECAUSE SHE HATED HER LIFE.
WHEN SHE CAME BACK
HE HAD A CHILD AND WIFE.

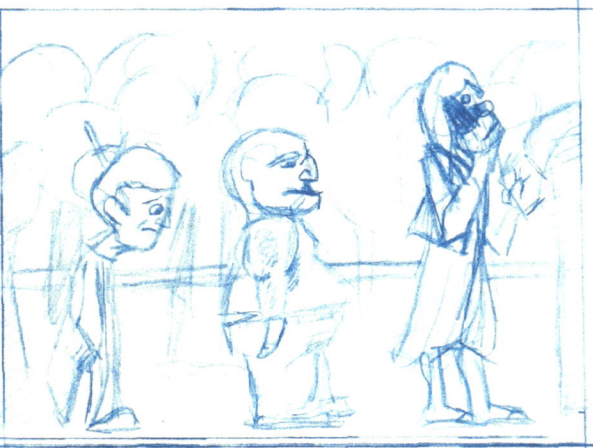

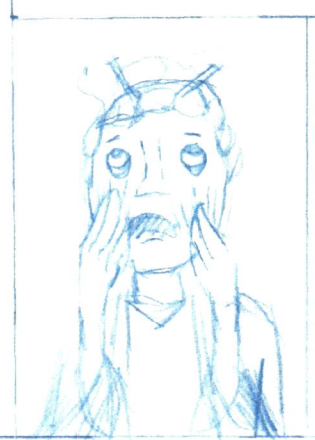
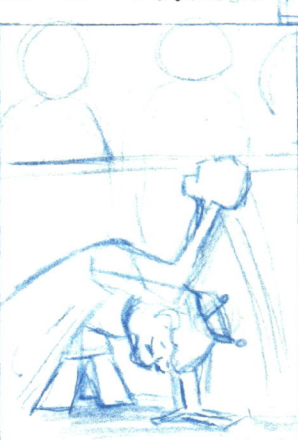
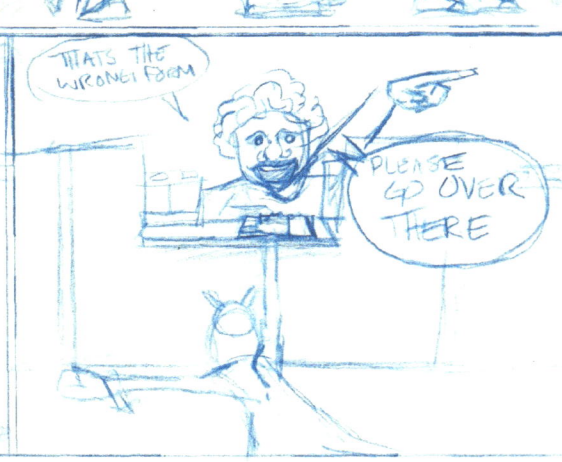

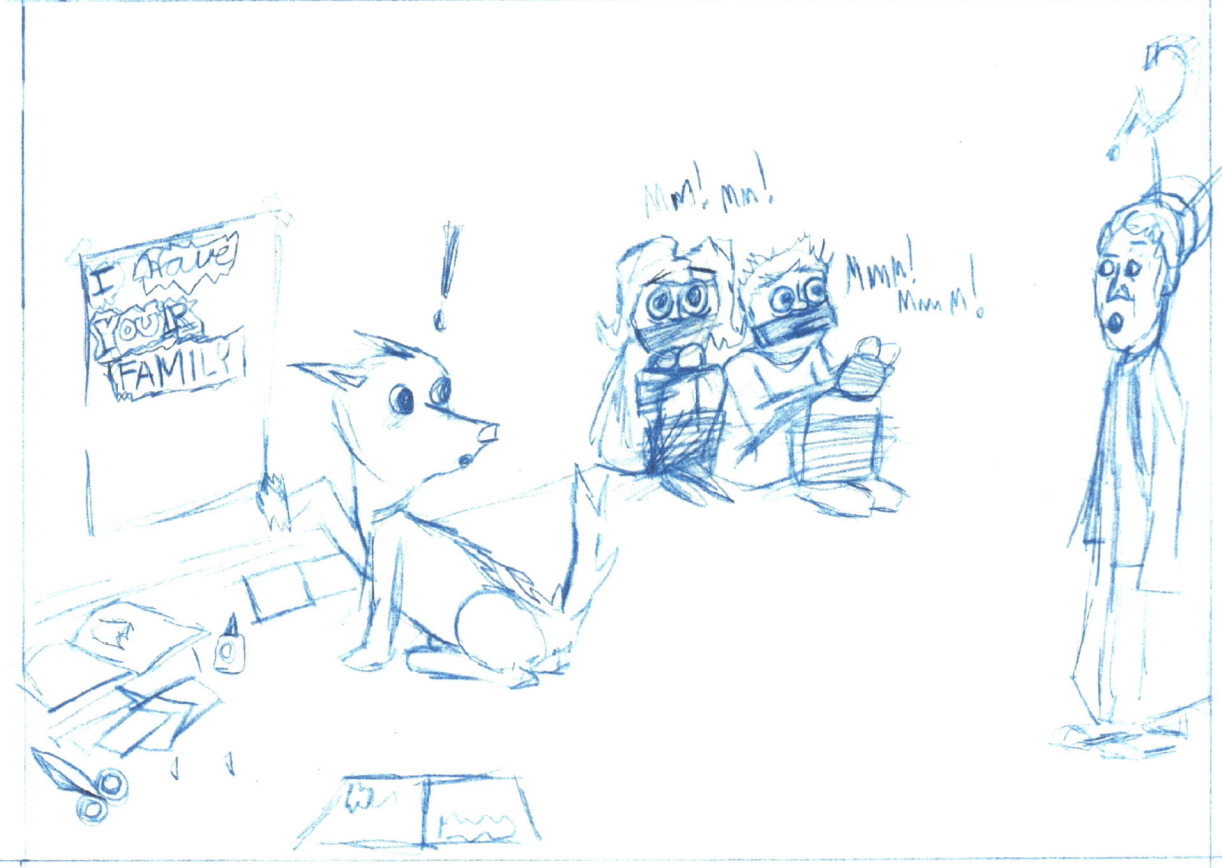

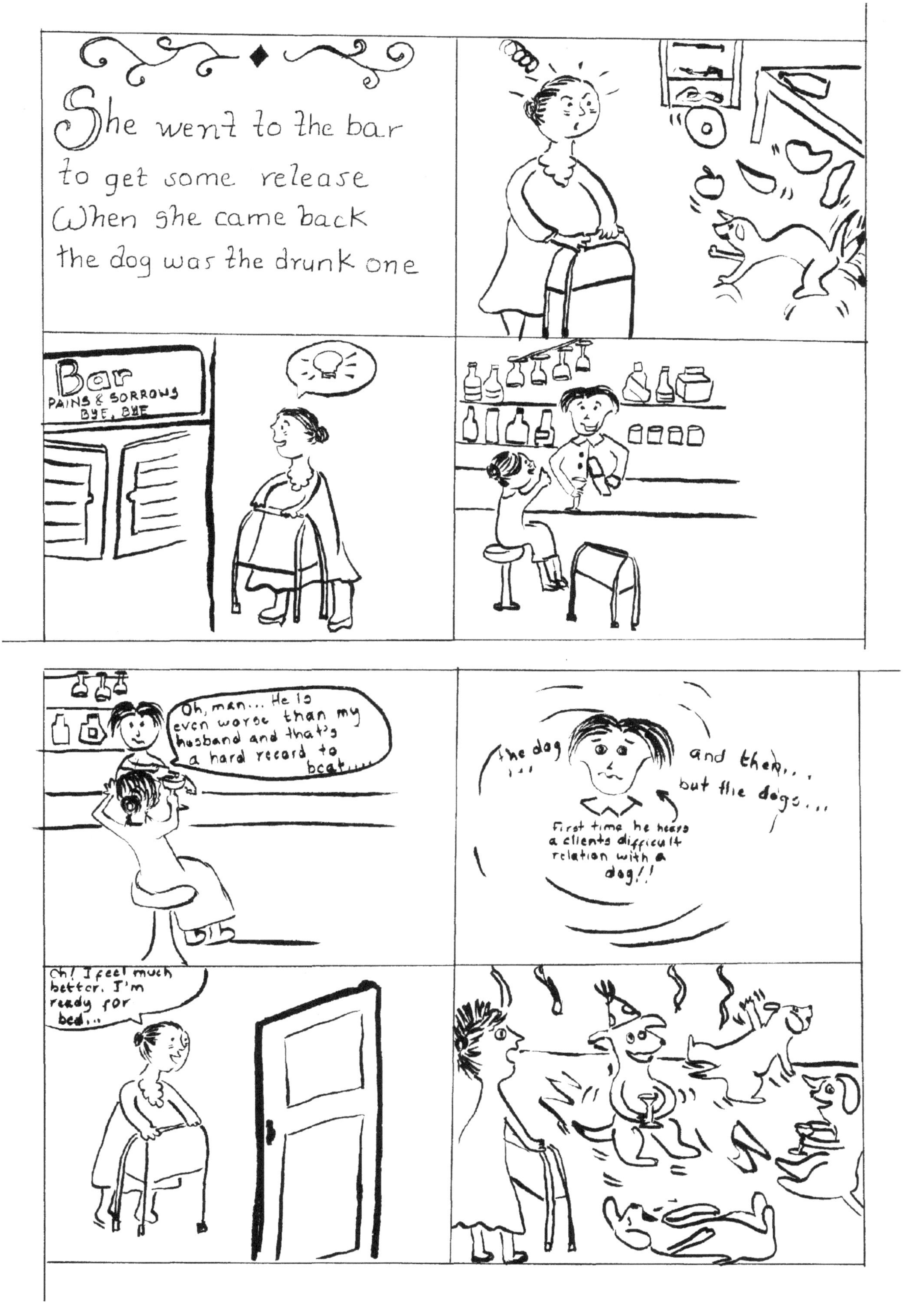
She went to the bar
to get some release
When she came back
the dog was the drunk one
Bar
PAINS & SORROWS
BYE, BYE
Oh, man... He is even worse than my husband and that's a hard record to beat...
the dog ...
and then...
but the dogs...
First time he hears a clients difficult relation with a dog!!
Oh! I feel much better. I'm ready for bed...

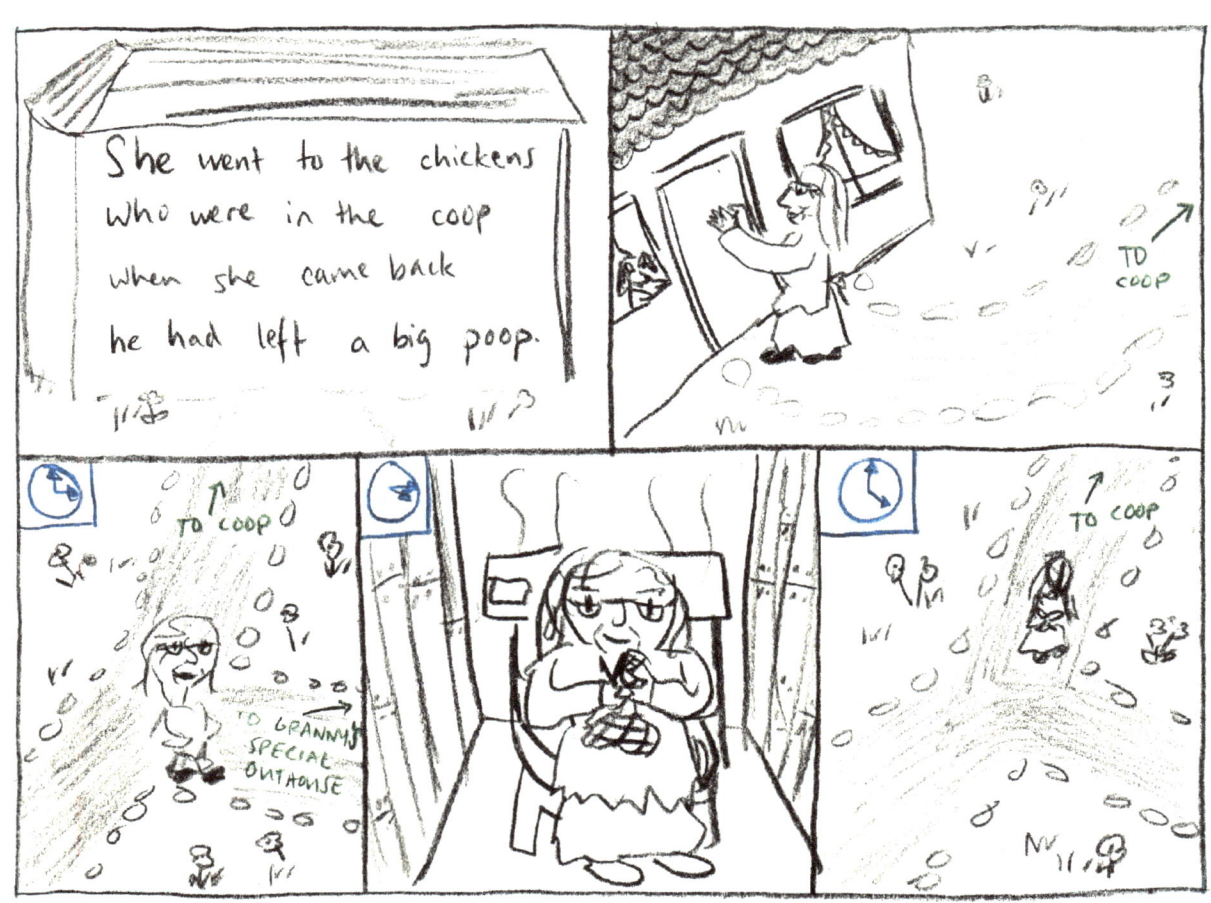

She went to the chickens
who were in the coop
when she came back
he had left a big poop.

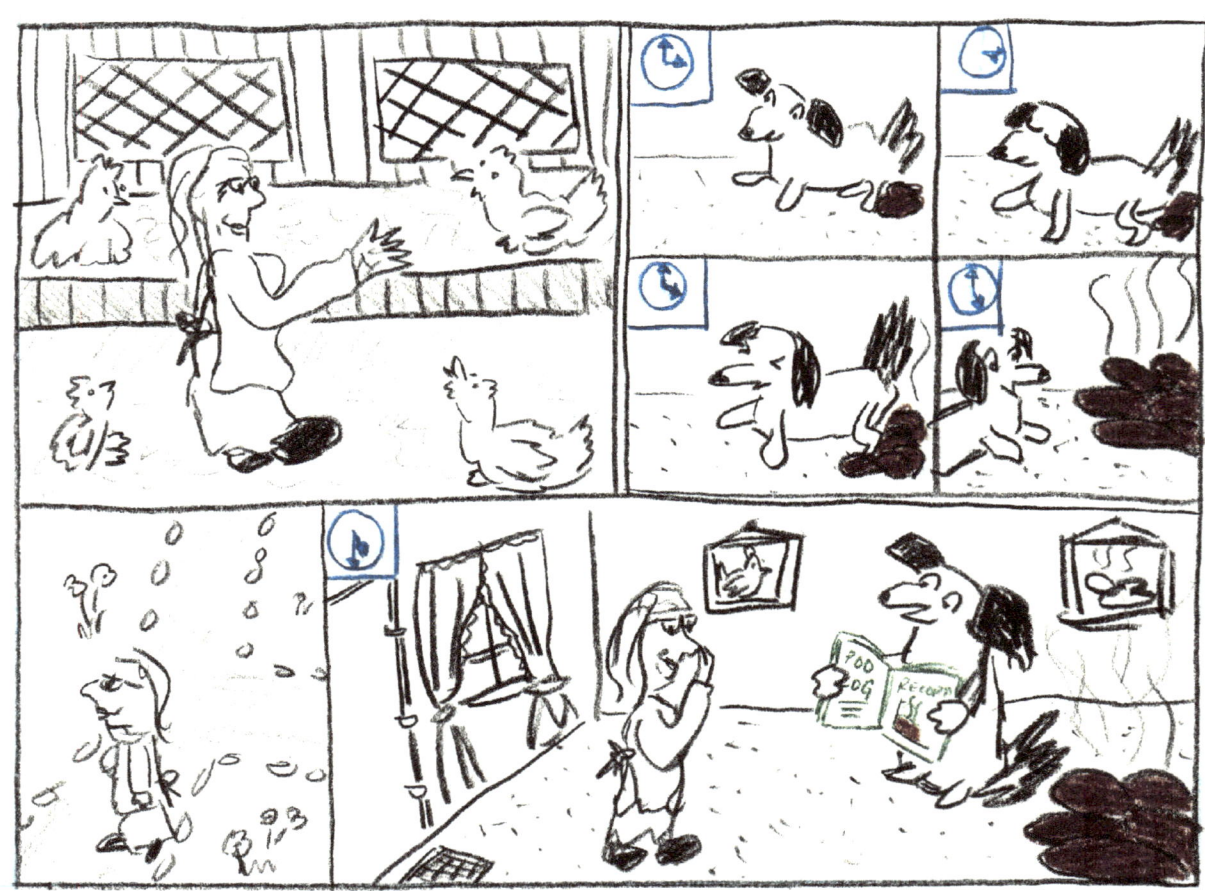

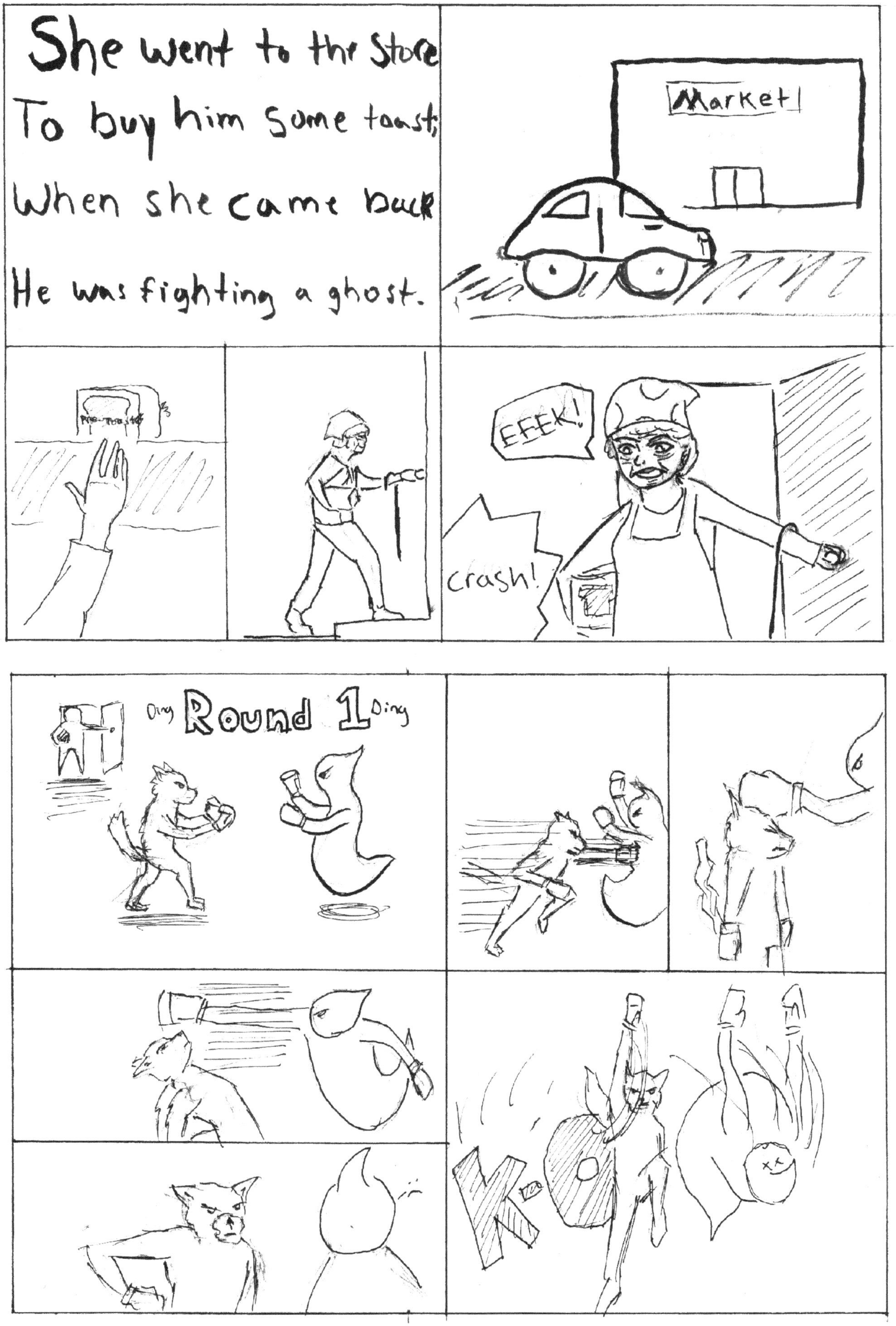
She went to the Store
To buy him some toast;
When she came back
He was fighting a ghost.
Market
EEEK!
crash!
Ding
Round 1
Ding

SHE WENT TO THE BAKER'S TO BUY HIM A PIE; WHEN SHE CAME BACK HE WAS LICKING A FLY.

which would you like, ma'am?

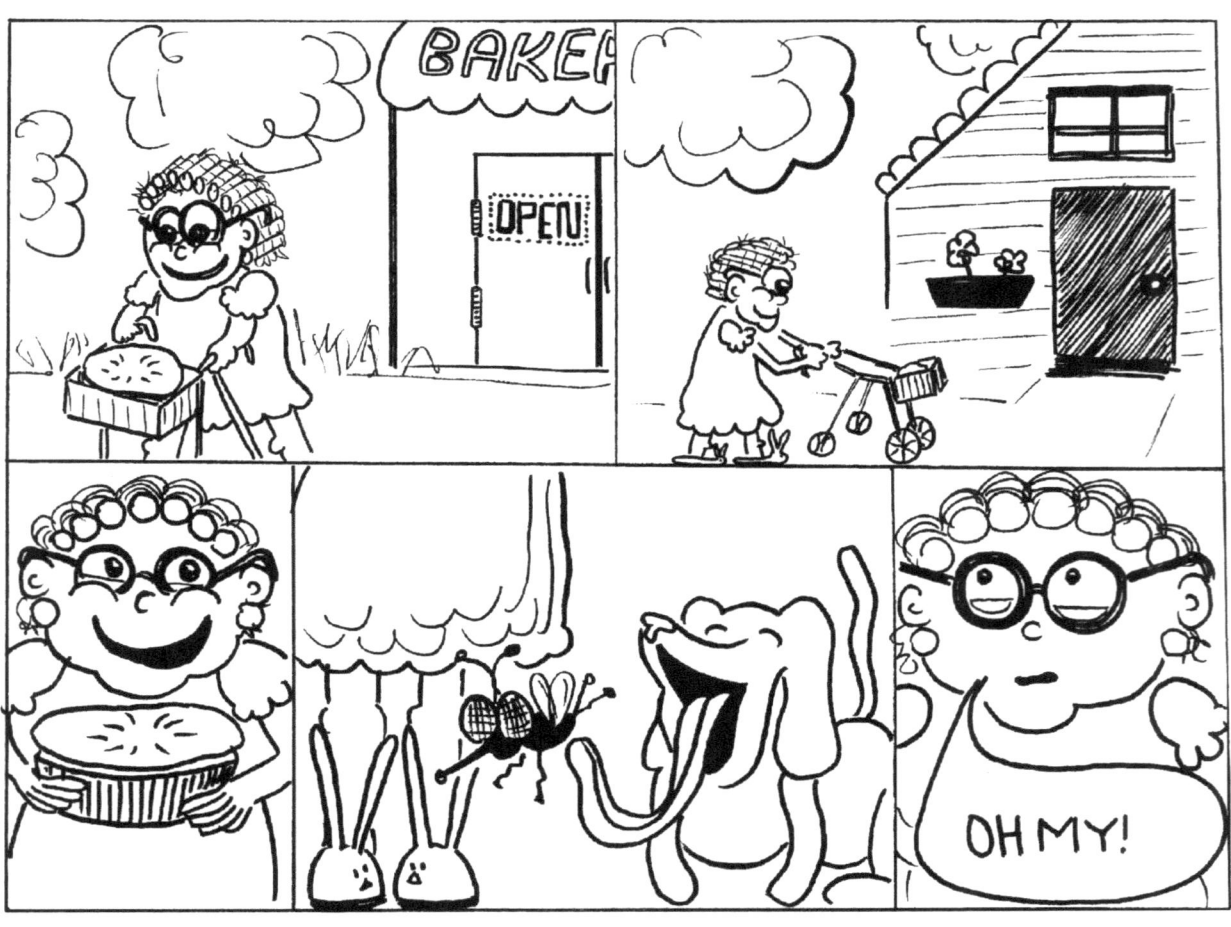

OH MY!

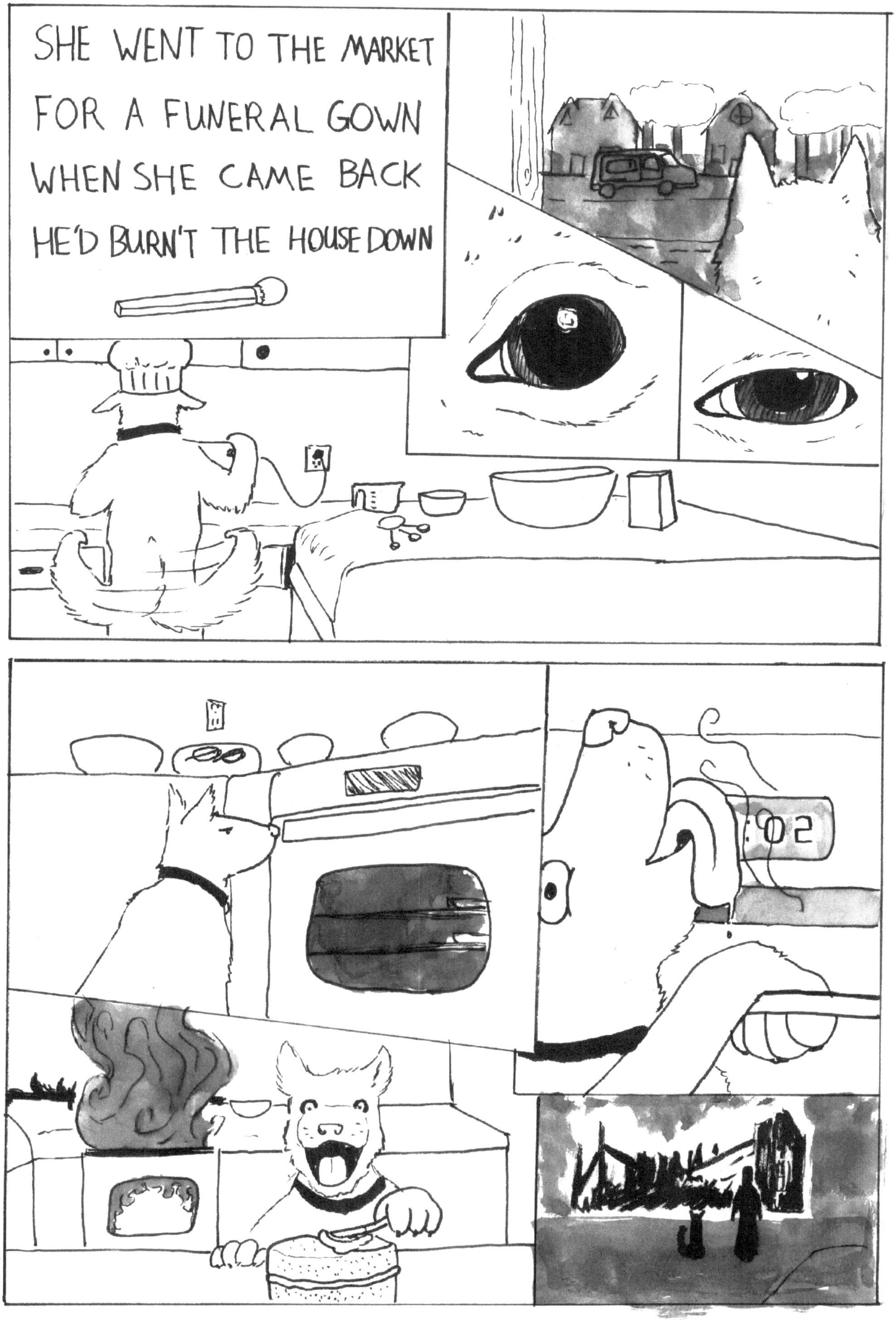
SHE WENT TO THE MARKET
FOR A FUNERAL GOWN
WHEN SHE CAME BACK
HE'D BURN'T THE HOUSE DOWN
:02

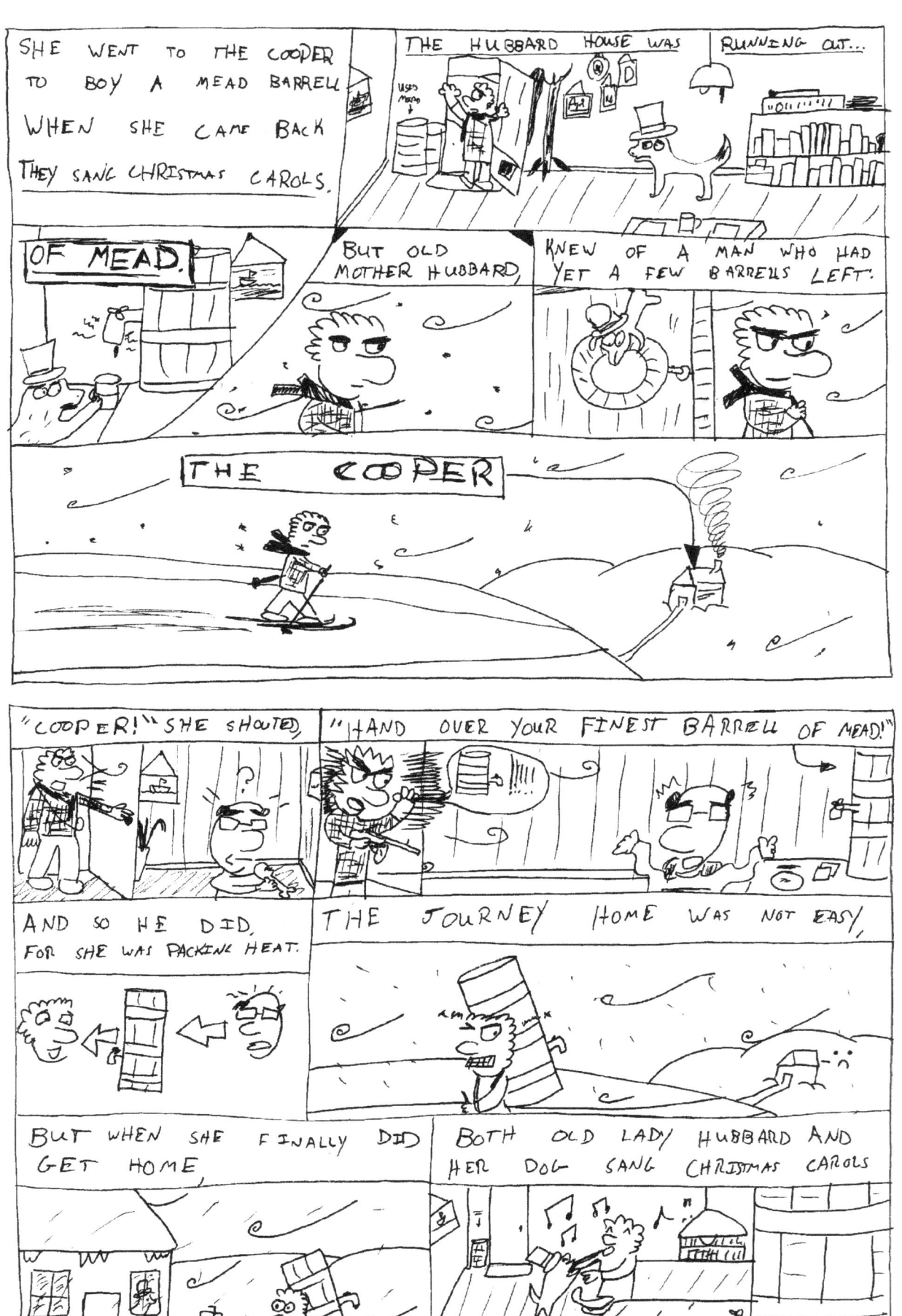

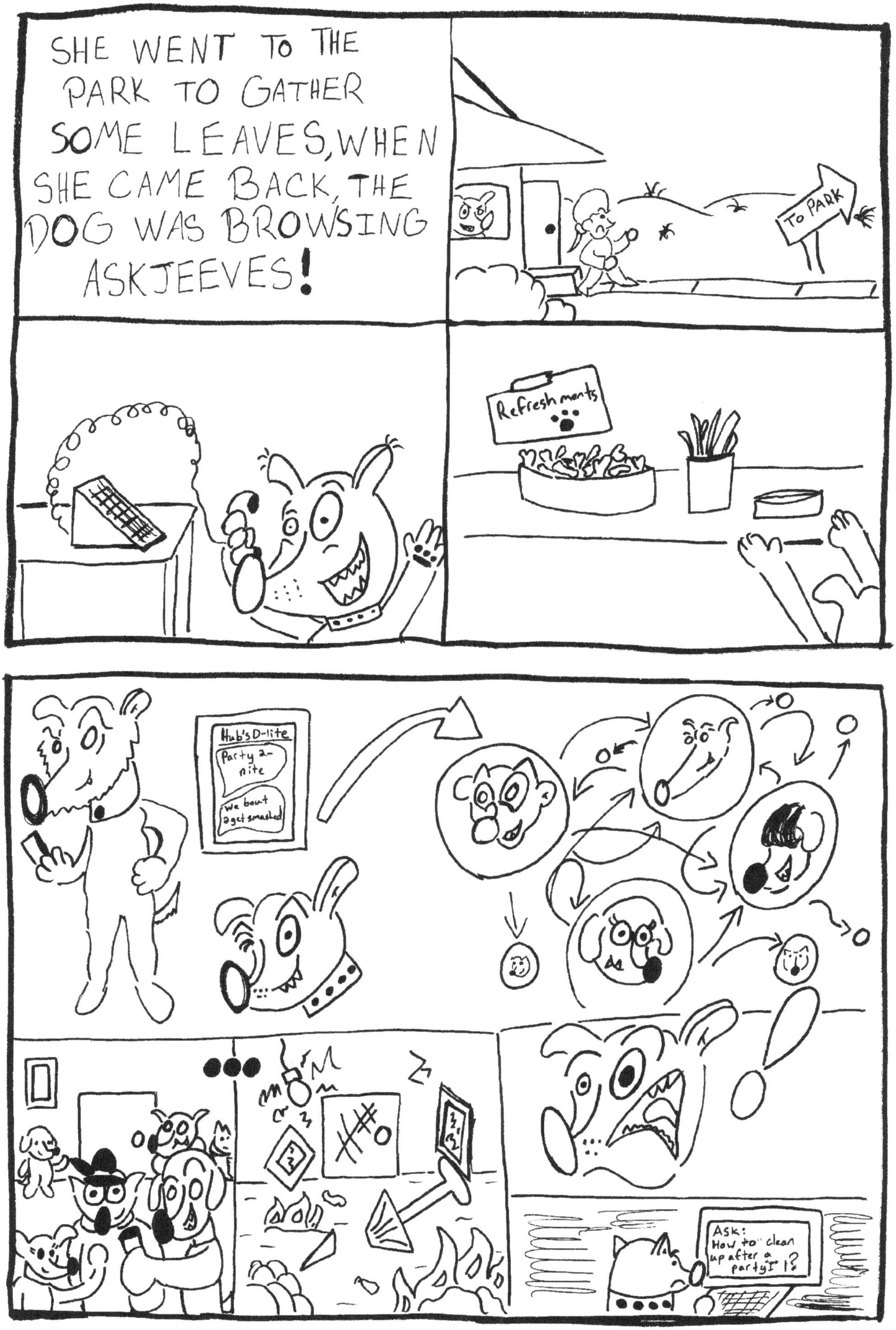
SHE WENT TO THE PARK TO GATHER SOME LEAVES, WHEN SHE CAME BACK, THE DOG WAS BROWSING ASKJEEVES!
TO PARK
Refreshments
Hub's D-lite
Party 2-nite
We bout 2 get smashed
Ask: How to clean up after a party!?

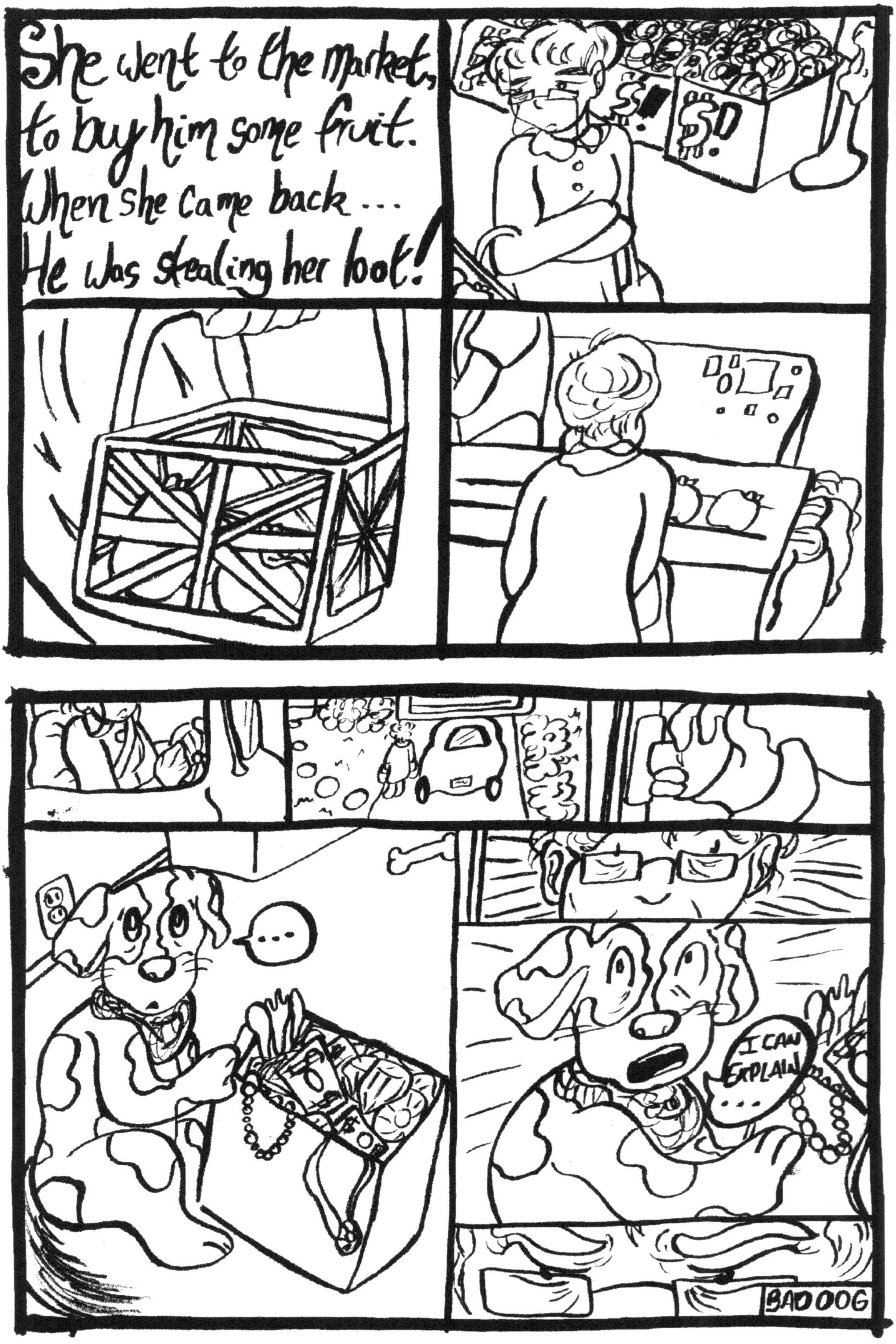

She went to the market, to buy him some fruit. When she came back ... He was stealing her loot!

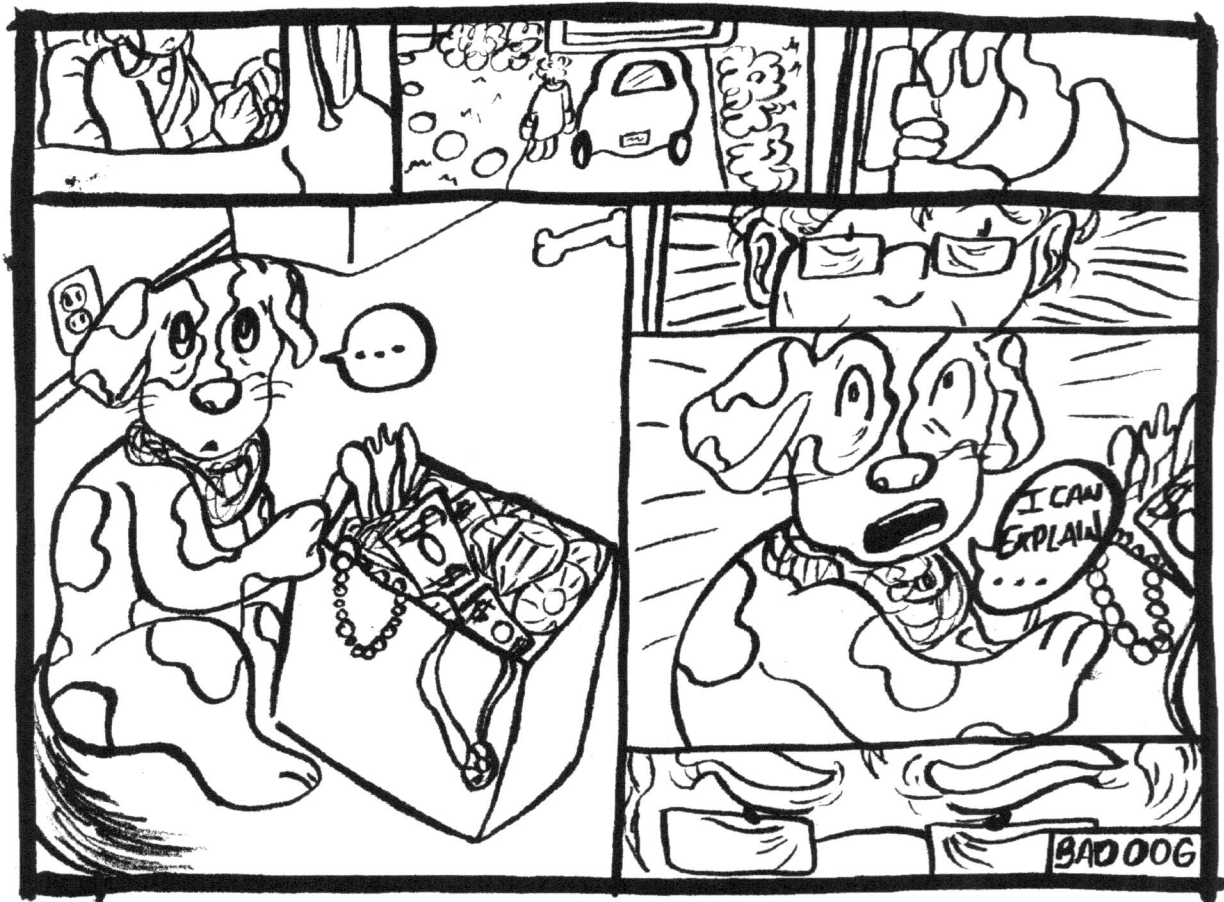

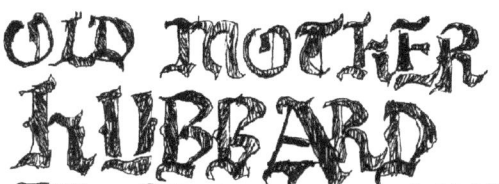
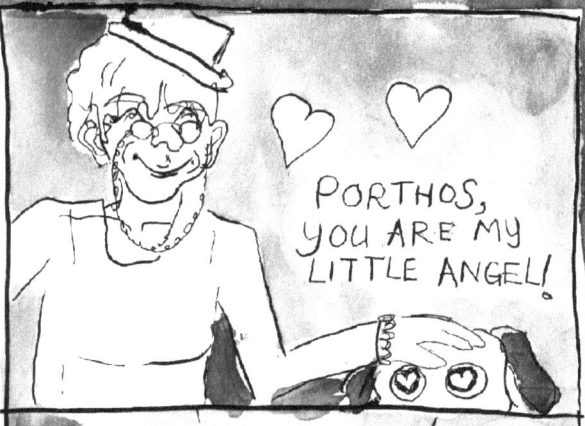
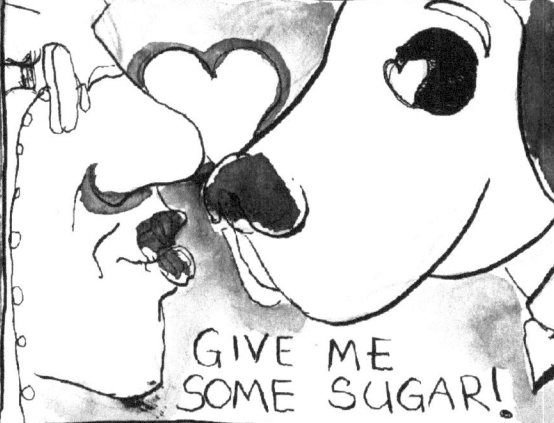
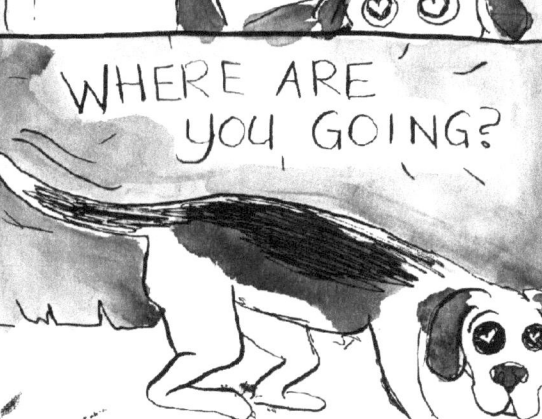
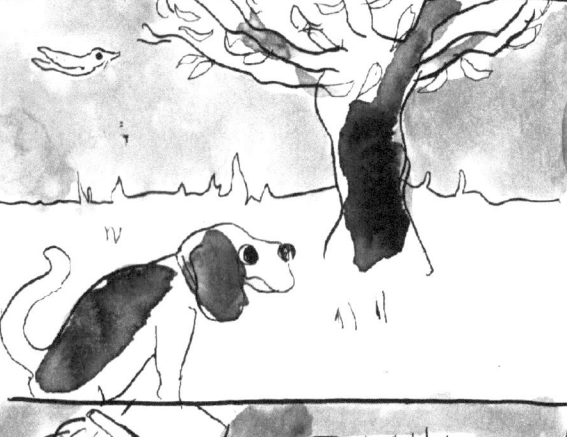
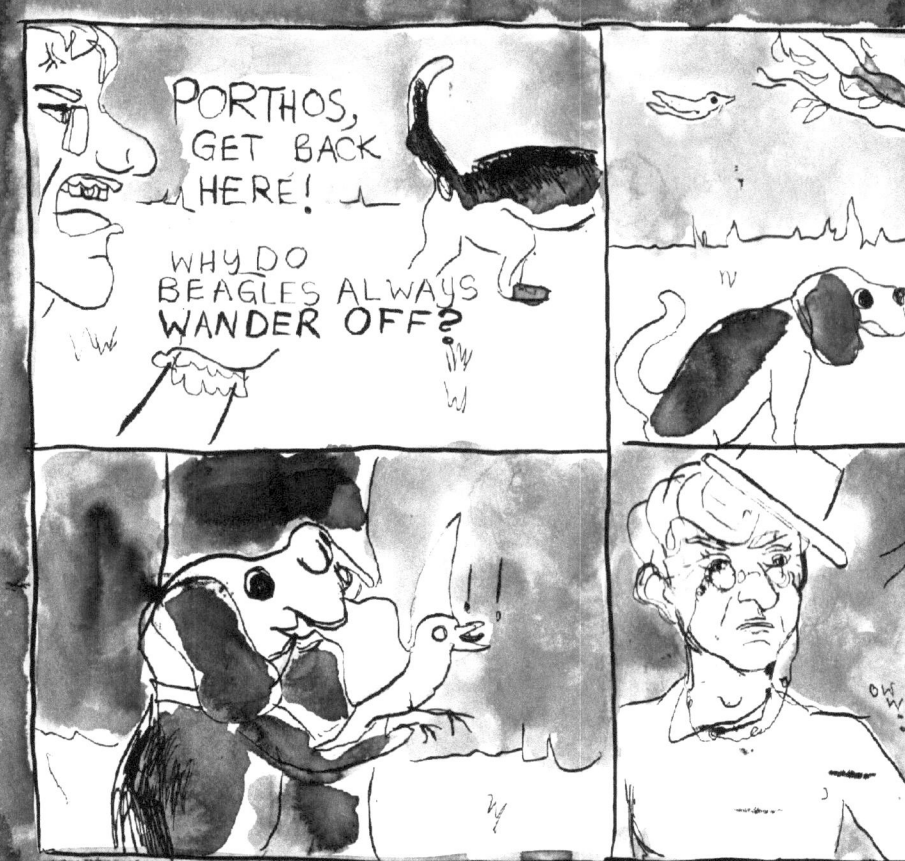
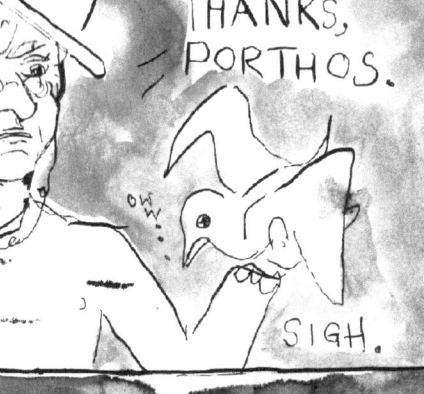

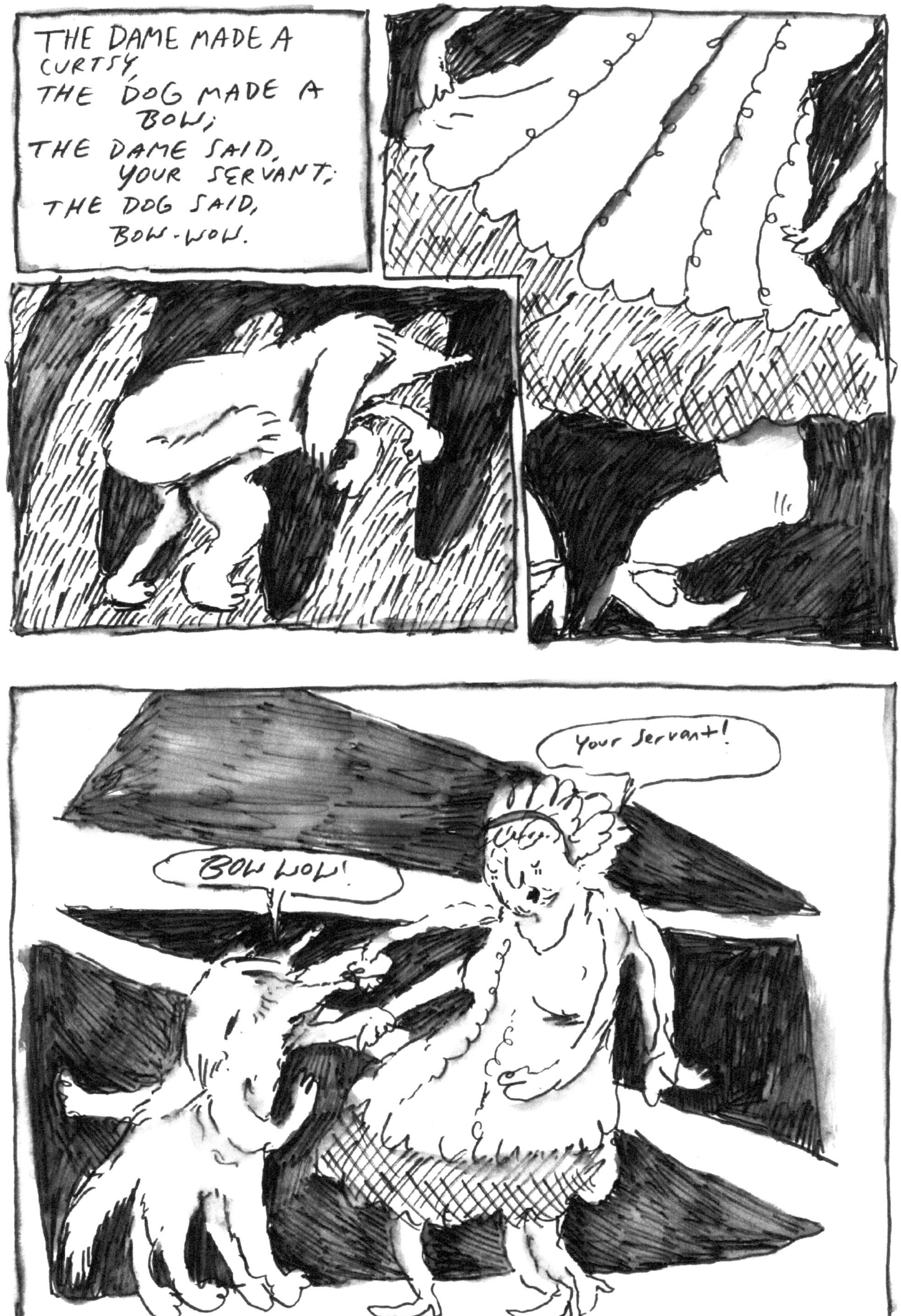

THE DAME MADE A
CURTSY,
THE DOG MADE A
BOW;
THE DAME SAID,
   YOUR SERVANT;
THE DOG SAID,
   BOW-WOW.

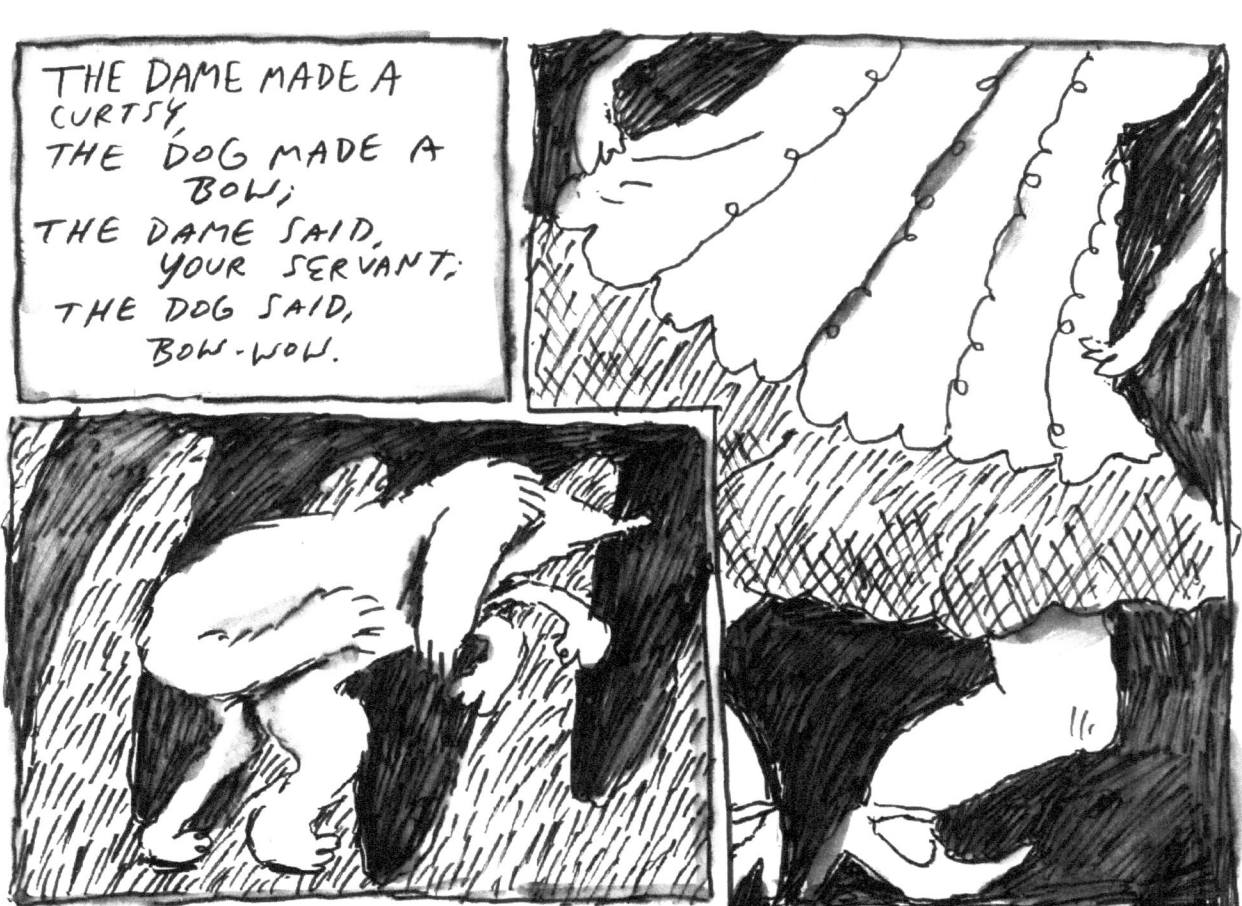

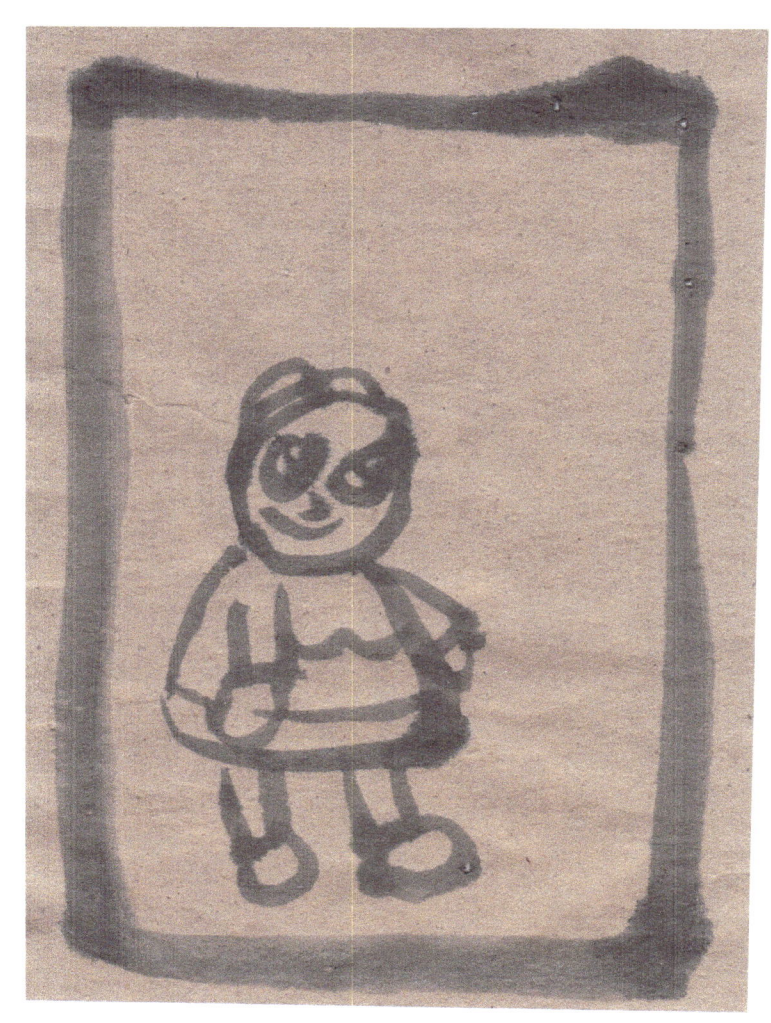

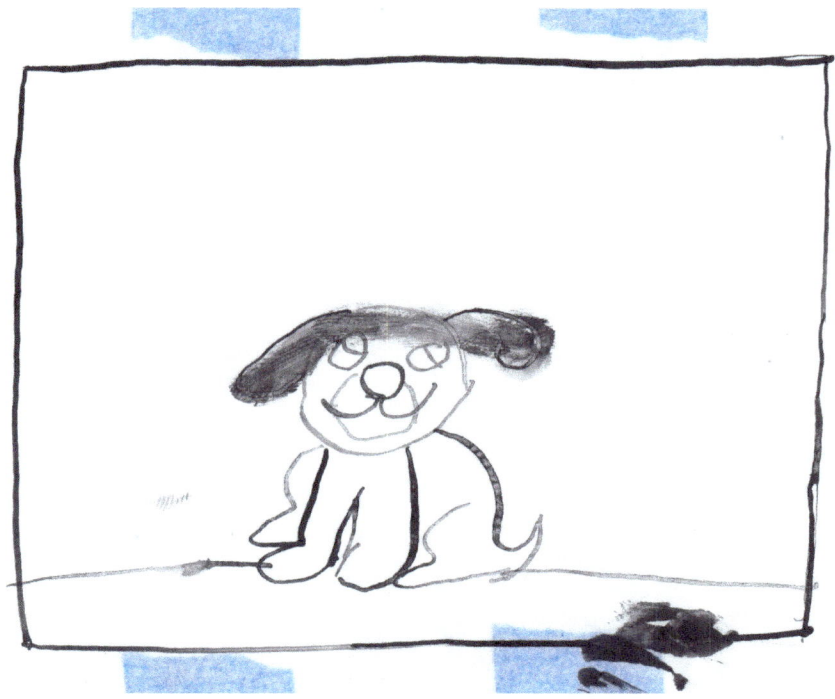

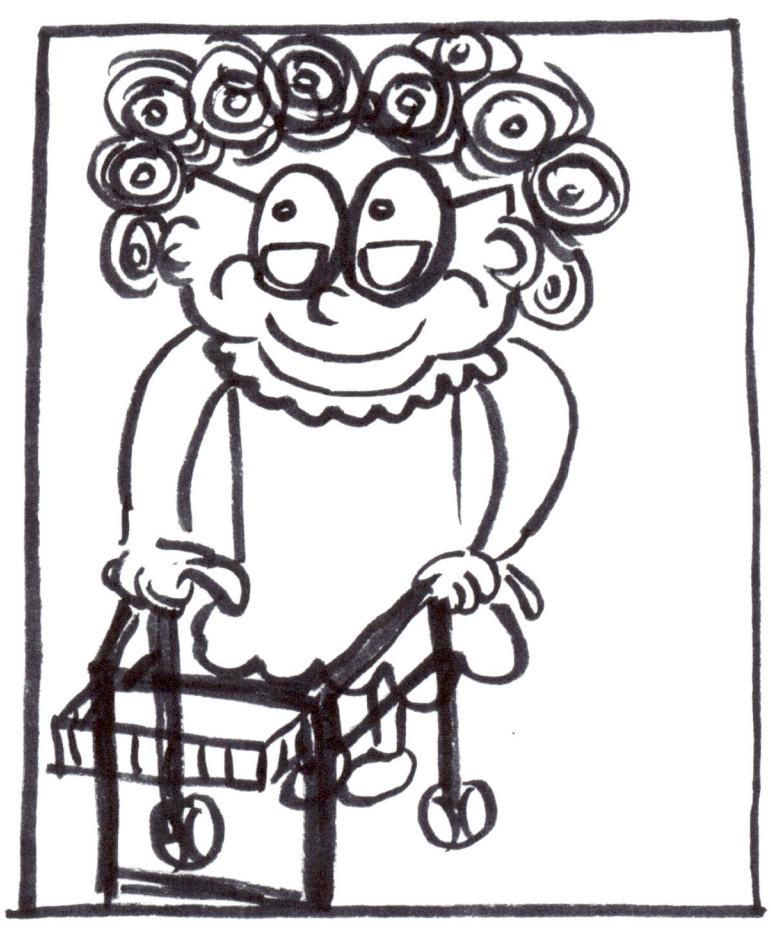

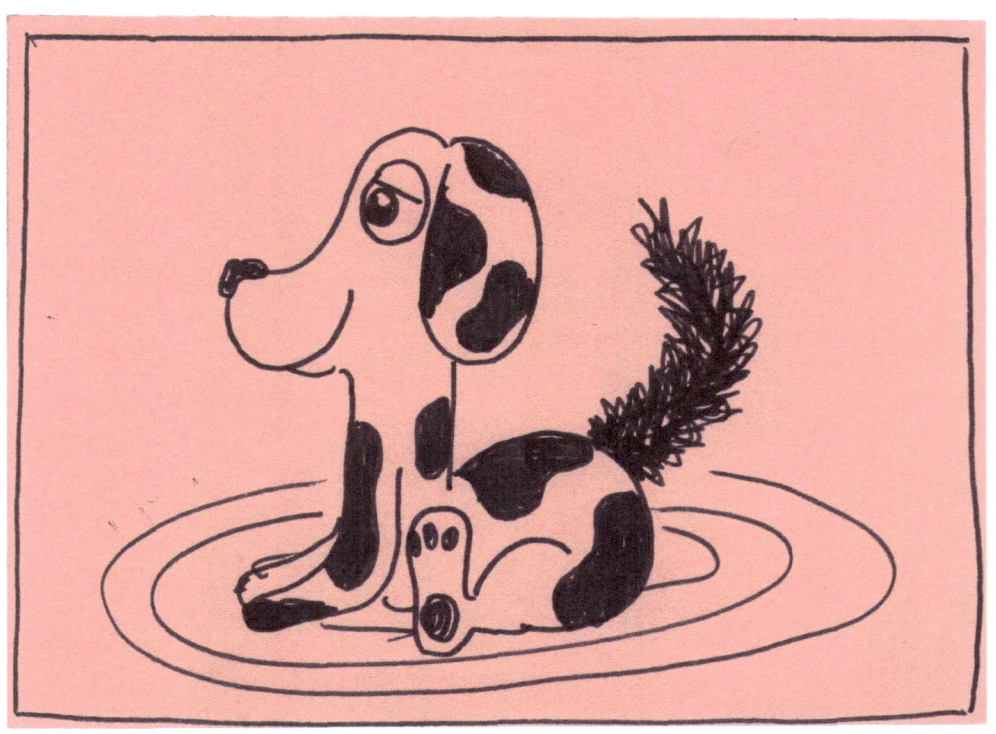

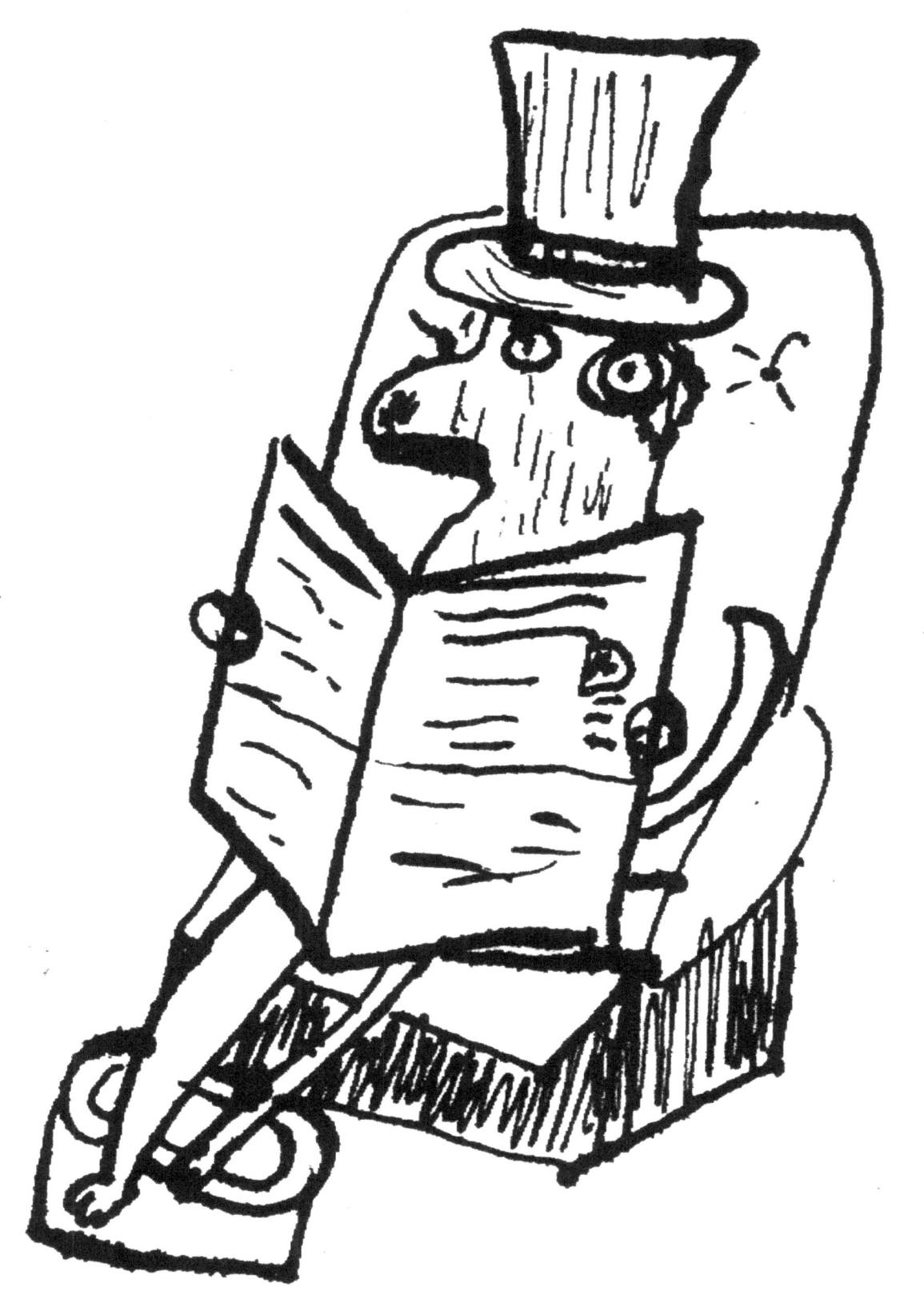

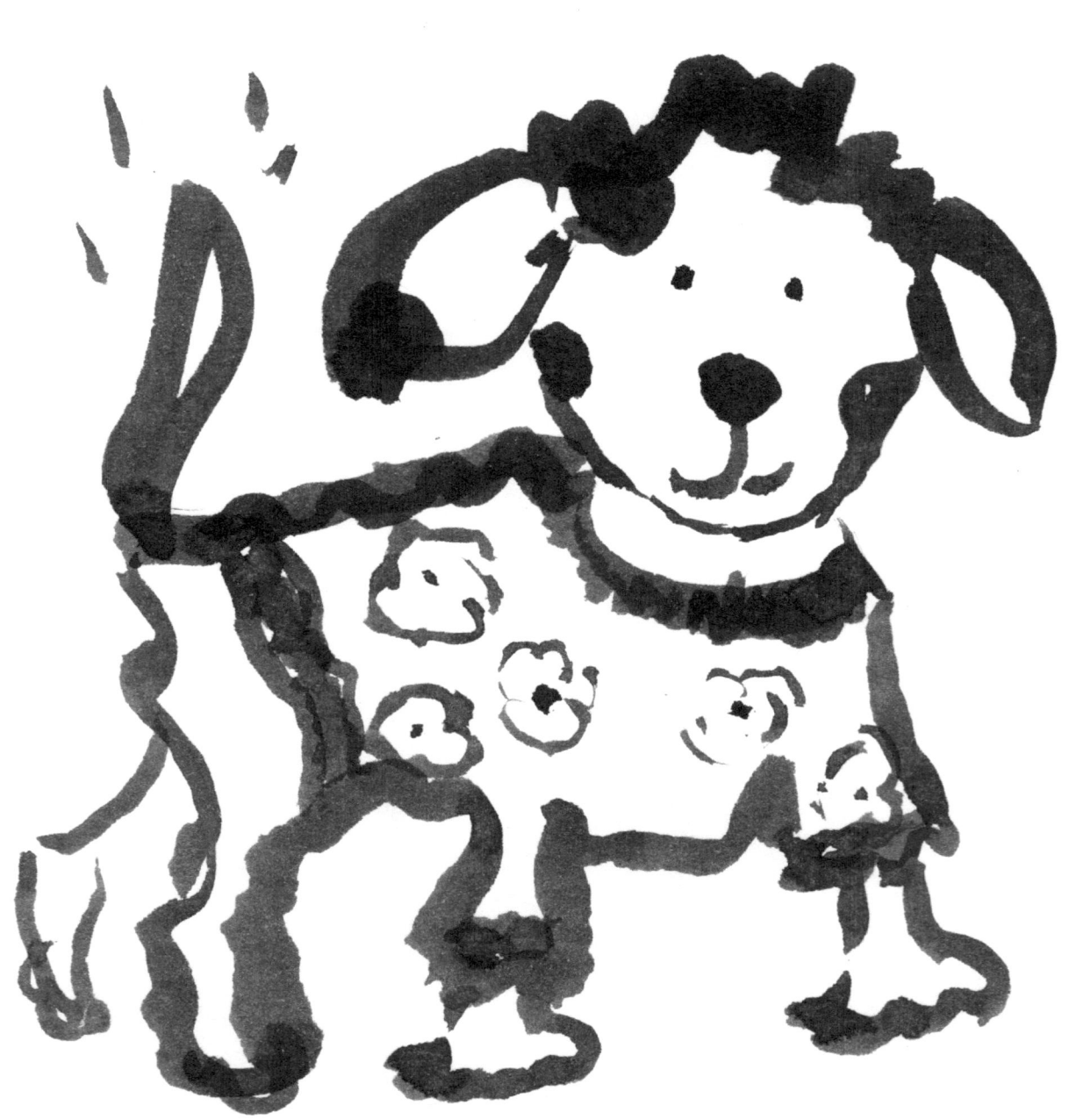

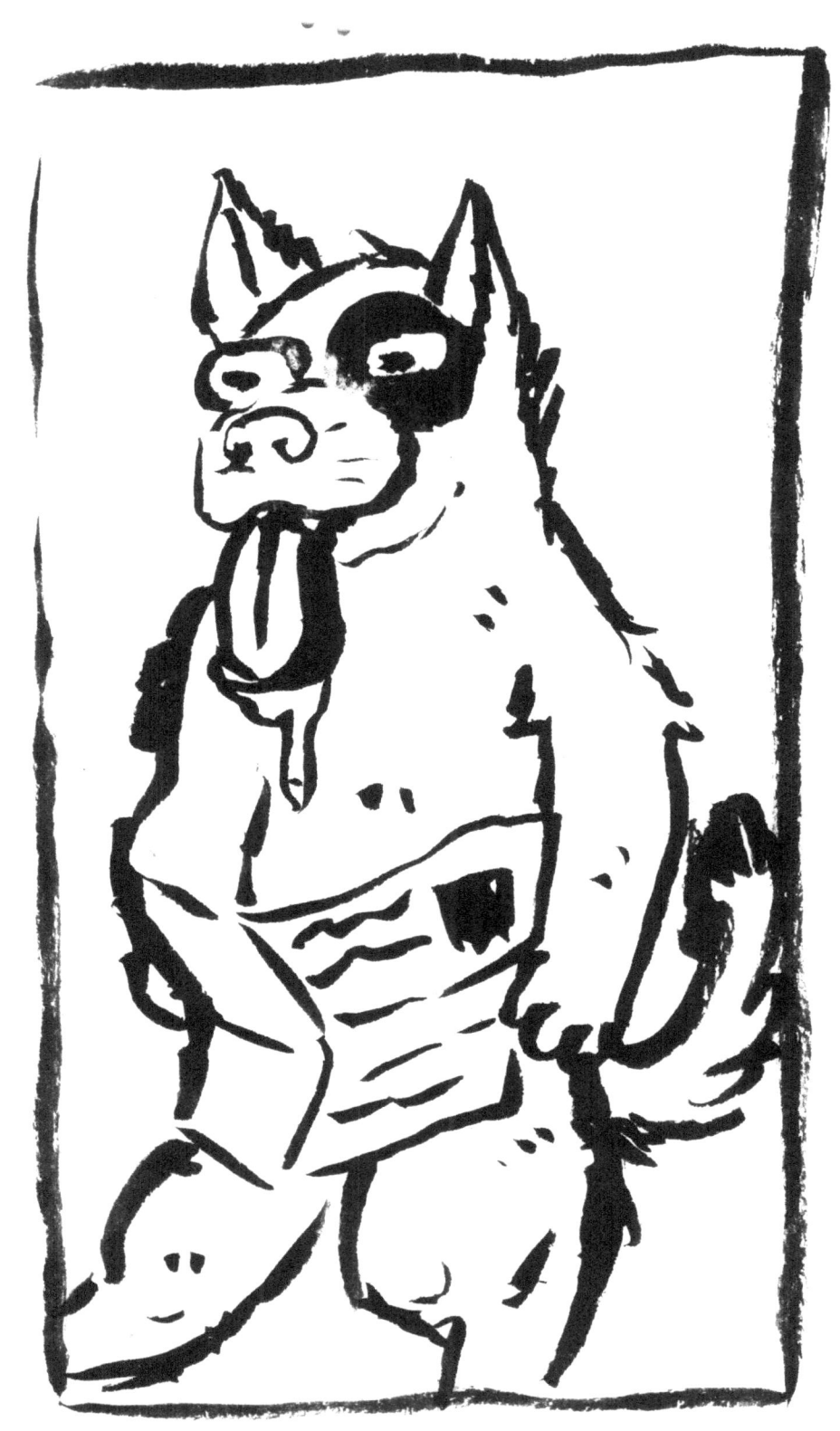

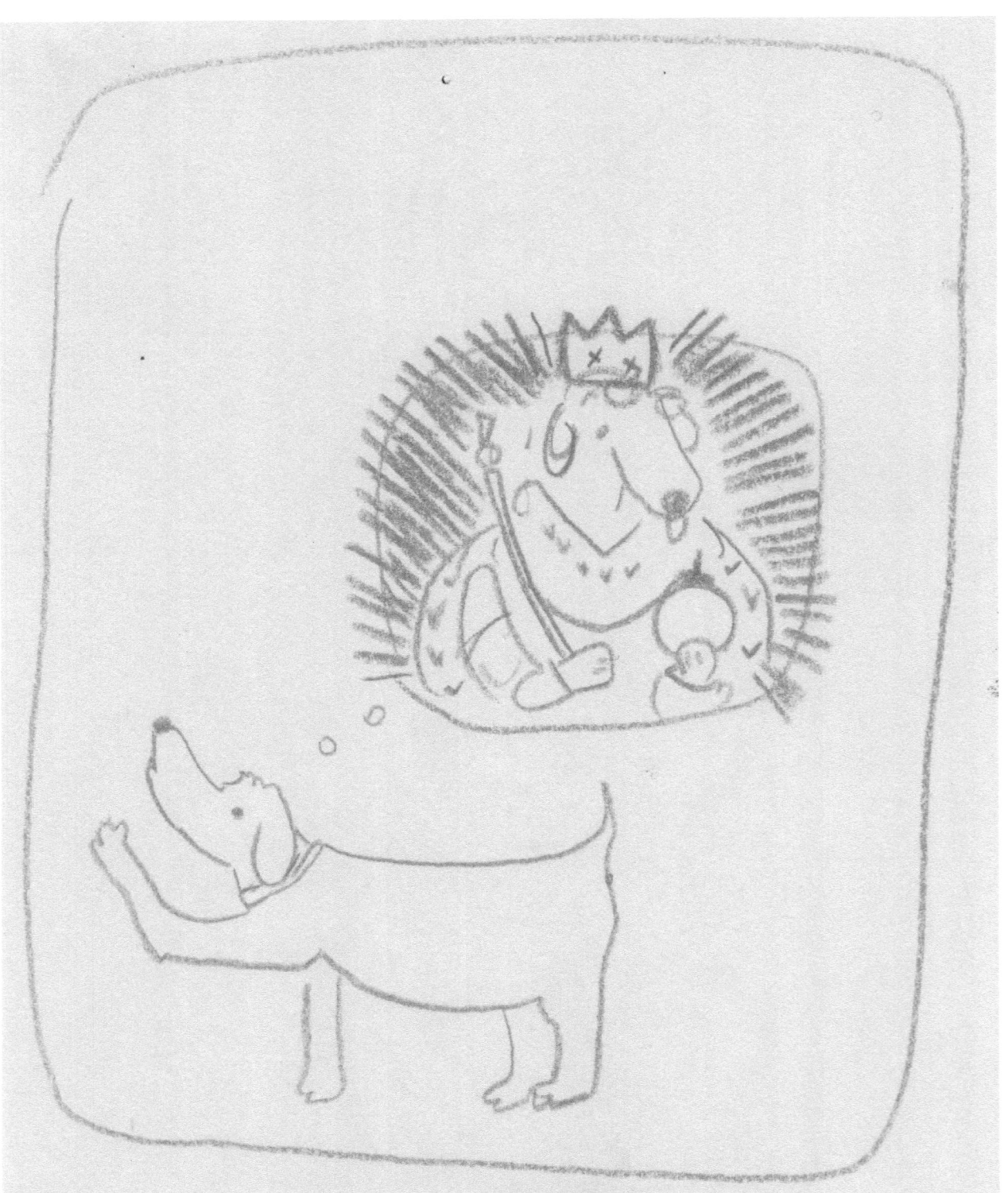

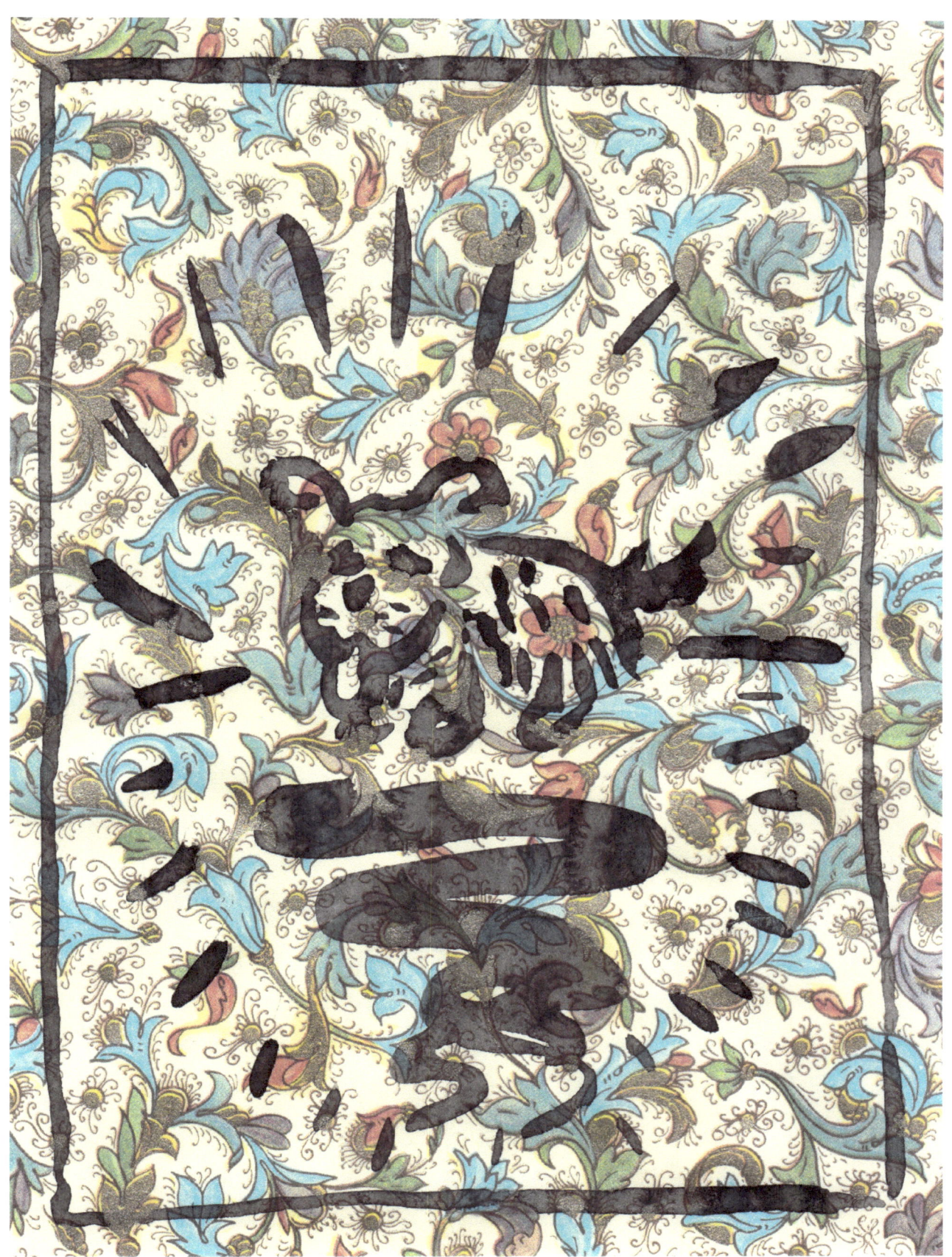

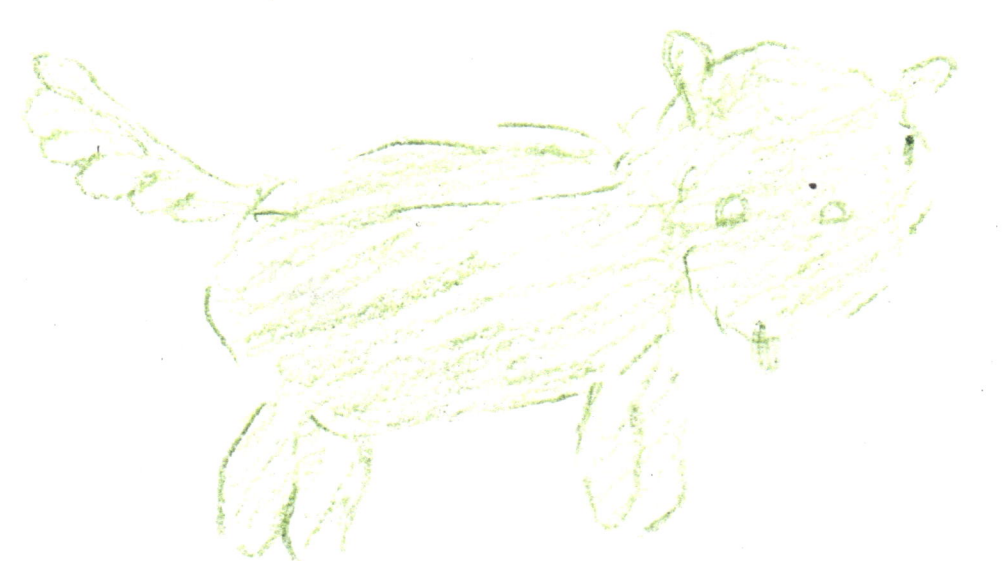

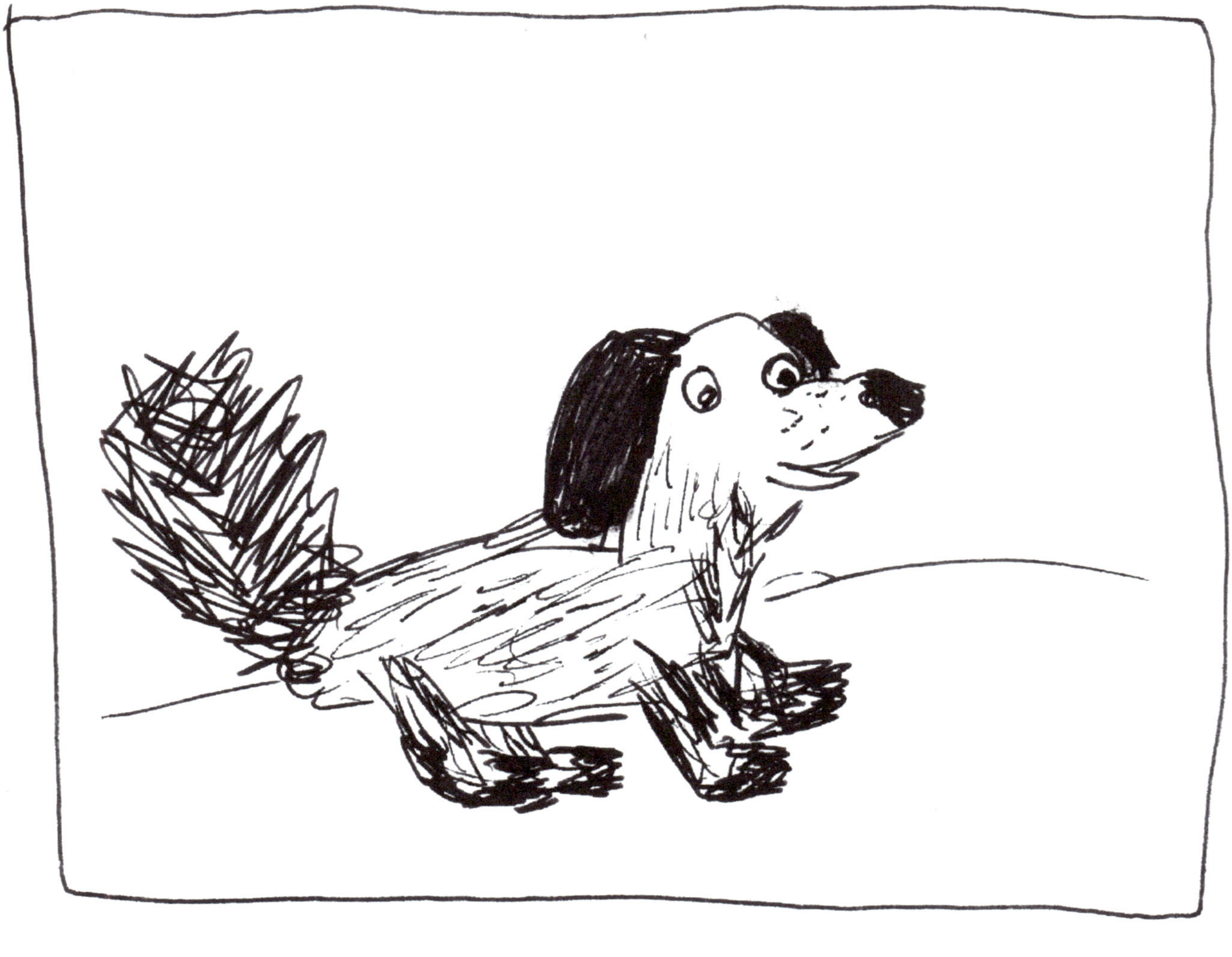

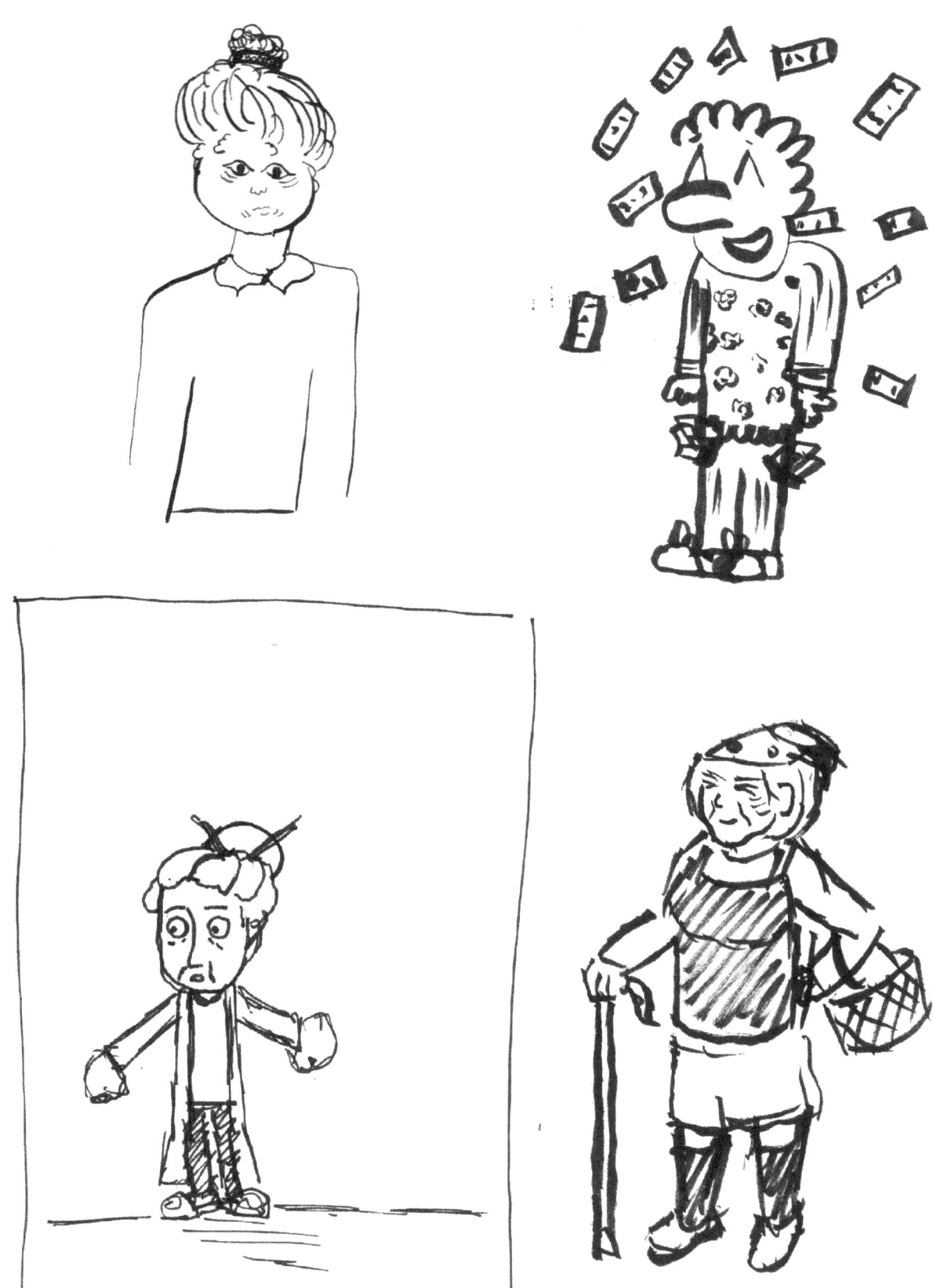

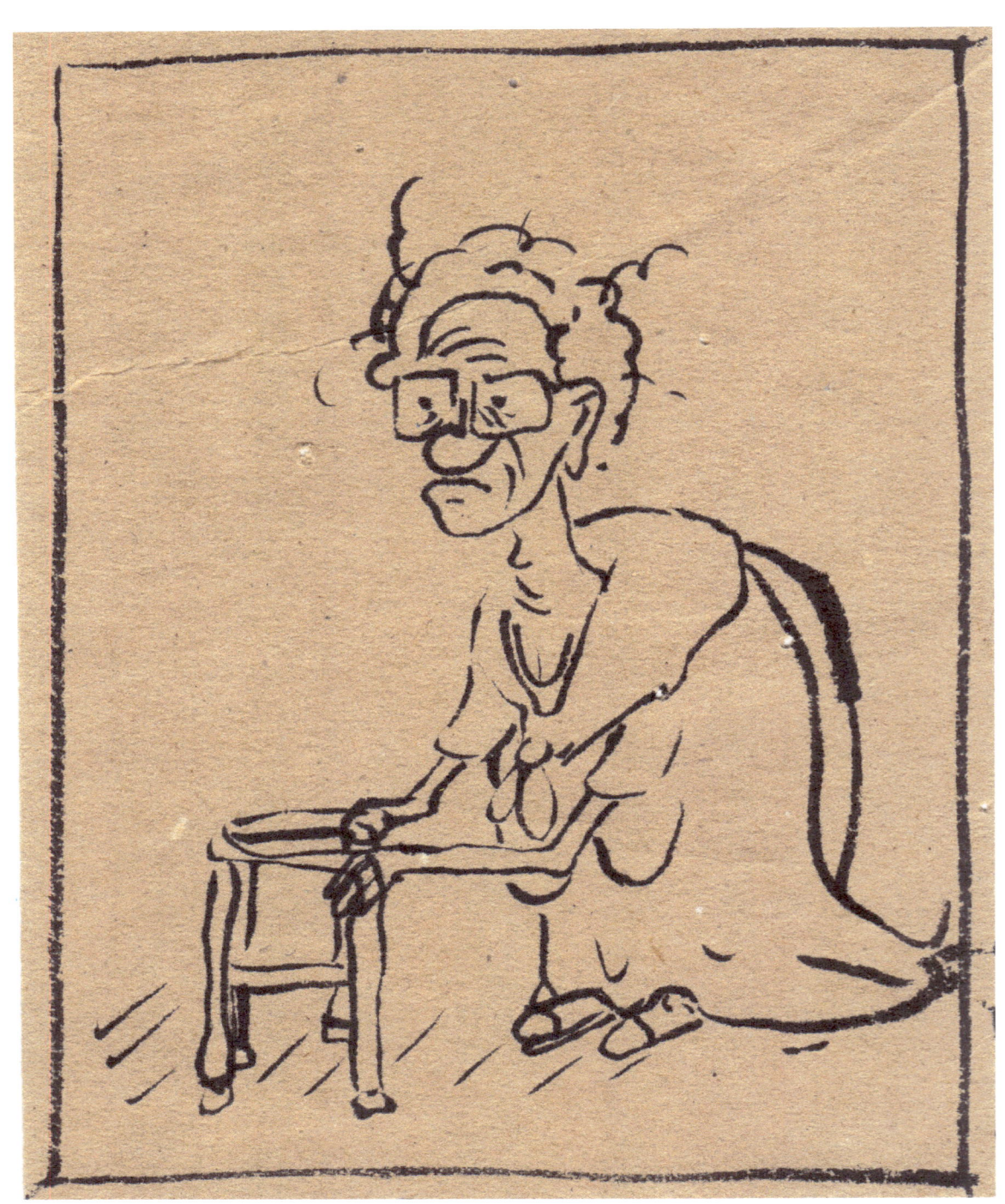

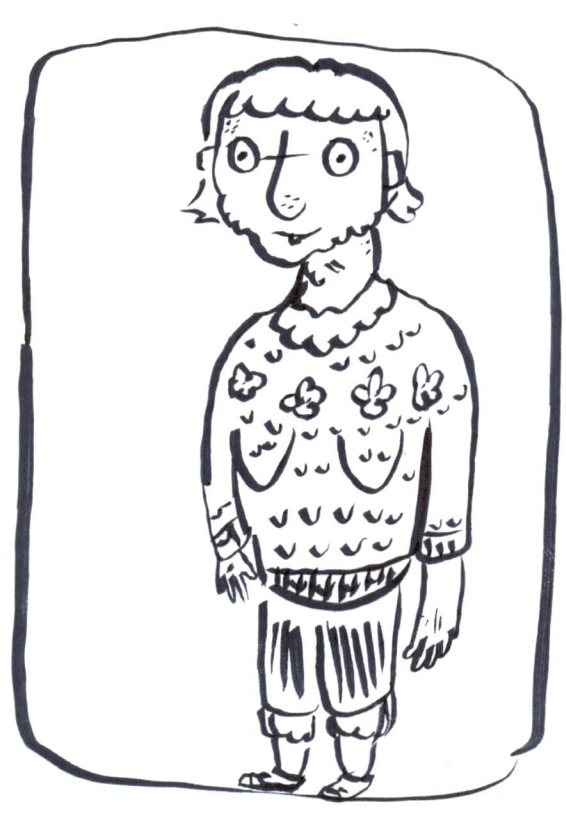
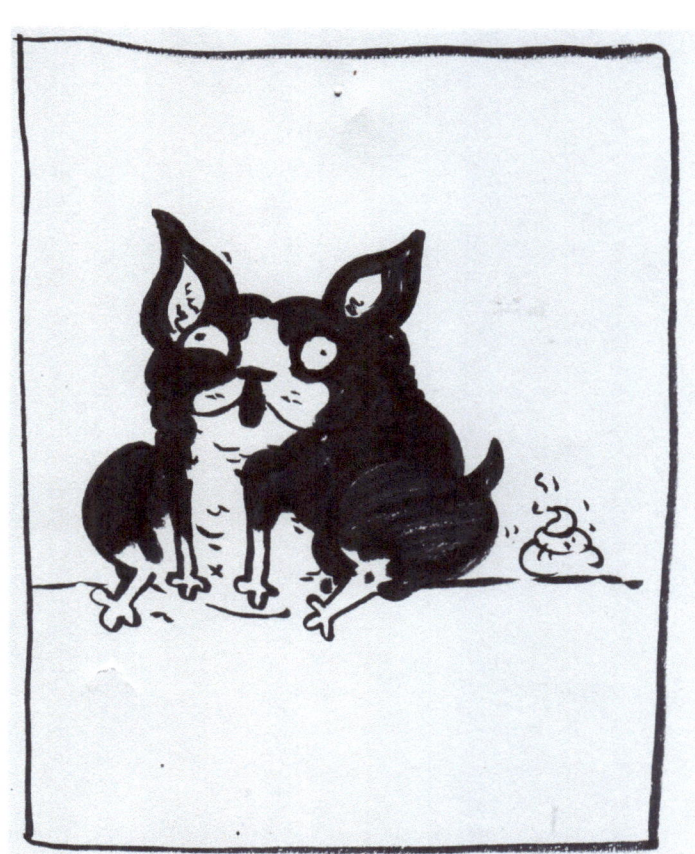
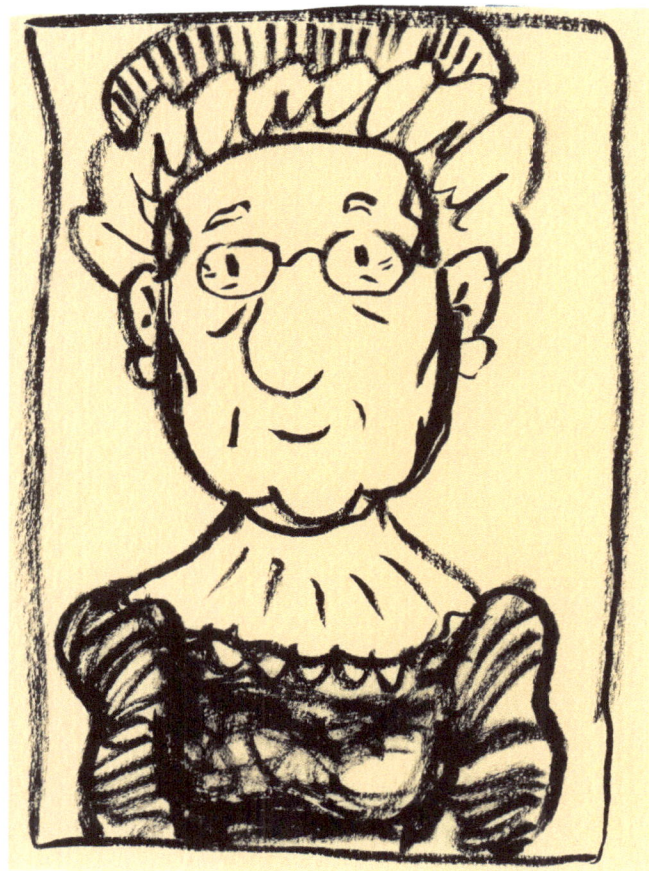
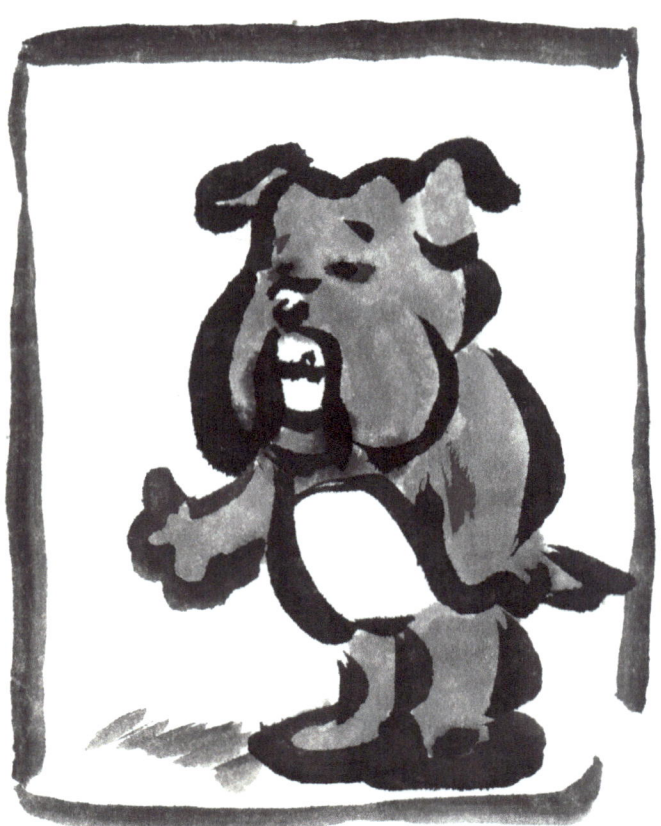

www.ingramcontent.com/pod-product-compliance
Lightning Source LLC
Chambersburg PA
CBHW050413180526
45159CB00005B/2259